CHANGE OR DIE

CHANGE OR DIE

*How to Transform Your
Organization from the Inside Out*

M. David Dealy
with Andrew R. Thomas

Westport, Connecticut
London

Library of Congress Cataloging-in-Publication Data

Dealy, M. David.
  Change or die : how to transform your organization from the inside out /
M. David Dealy with Andrew R. Thomas.
      p.   cm.
  Includes bibliographical references.
  ISBN: 978-0-313-36192-0
1. Organizational change.   I. Thomas, Andrew R.   II. Title.
HD58.8.D425   2006
658.4'02—dc22   2005019181

British Library Cataloguing in Publication Data is available.

Library of Congress Catalog Card Number: 2005019181
ISBN: 978-0-313-36192-0

First published in 2006

Praeger Publishers, 88 Post Road West, Westport, CT 06881
An imprint of Greenwood Publishing Group, Inc.
www.praeger.com

Printed in the United States of America

The paper used in this book complies with the
Permanent Paper Standard issued by the National
Information Standards Organization (Z39.48–1984).

10 9 8 7 6 5 4 3 2 1

For my wife, Karen
—M. David Dealy

Contents

Chapter 1

The Inevitability
of Change

Nothing endures but change.
Heraclites

ALTHOUGH IT WAS 20 years ago, it seems like just yesterday. Life was good. After 8 years with the company, I was promoted to a job with a big title and even bigger salary. Everything seemed to be going my way until that day when my boss, the general manager, called me into his office.

I felt that I could handle anything. I had started at the bottom and worked my way up. In the railroad business that meant working on the track with large gangs of other guys who also started at the bottom. And it meant being outside all day long in the blistering heat of summer and the painful cold of winter. We rebuilt track by replacing creosoted cross ties and steel rail. It was hard work, with long hours that left little time for anything else.

Fortunate enough to be promoted from job to job, I had established myself as a "change agent." I don't think the term had been coined yet, but that is what I was. The common questions on audit trips by senior management always revolved around what I had changed lately, how it was working, and what was I looking at changing next. The company believed that if you were to improve, it had to be done through change. If you did not initiate and implement change, you became invisible. When you became invisible, you were ineffective. When you were ineffective, your career would stagnate and you would soon be unemployed.

This company had recently operated itself out of receivership, a sort of bankruptcy for railroads, and was now doing quite well. Four years after joining the company, we were purchased by a much larger, more profitable railroad whose culture and attitude embodied everything except change. Two years after we were sold, I was promoted to the position of general superintendent in the home turf of the company that had acquired us. We were treated cordially, but more like second-class citizens. After all, what could a rag-tag group of managers from a smaller company, recently out of receivership, do to improve a long-established icon in the industry?

"The general manager wants to see you" were the words from the office manager.

I was sitting in my nicely appointed office in the company's headquarters, reflecting on the situation I was in. I was 29 years old and was holding a job that usually went to managers in their mid-fifties. Successful throughout my term and known for results by creating change, I was often viewed as a dangerous outsider to my boss, peers, and subordinates. I was determined to overcome this challenge.

With the title of general superintendent, I had risen seven levels from the rank and file employee and long left the track gangs. There were still three layers between me and the chief executive officer (CEO). It was a big job with big responsibilities, but it was like being with a whole new company. It was like starting over. I had no allies, I had to create them. I had no respect, I had to earn it. My main talent was that of initiating, implementing, and leading change. Now, I was in a company that did not want to change. Why should they? Things were going well, they were making money. In fact, change could only mess things up.

In those days, railroads tended to be very formal, almost militaristic. While we did not salute our superior, we never addressed them by their first name. There was always a "Mister" preceding the name. We wore conservative, dark suits and white, long-sleeved shirts. We even wore hats when we were out on the railroad, serious felt dress hats that you hardly saw on anyone else but railroaders. And, even though we were a formal group, we usually took our suit coats off while sitting in our private office.

When I entered the general manager's office, I could sense a serious conversation coming, as he was sitting with his suit coat on. Until then, I had been known as a good manager. I had tried many new things, most of which worked. The common remark made about me by senior management was, "Dave, even if he does fail from time to time, he never makes the same mistake twice . . . never." This was a tremendous amount of support that motivated me to try new things without worrying about an occasional failure. Rarely did any of my failures result to a level worse than before the change, and we could always revert back to the previous way of doing things. And I never made the same mistake twice.

Not only did the general manager have his suit coat on, but he also made a point of calling his office manager to come in and pour his cup of coffee, not offering any to me. He had to clear his throat several times as he spoke. When the words started rolling out of his mouth, a wave of shock began to set over me.

"Dave, we need to have a serious conversation," he started. Then he fumbled through his top drawer for a cigarette, lit it, and took a long draw, looked down at his desk, and then started again.

"Dave, we need to have a serious talk. I know that you were very successful on your previous assignments with the other company, but I believe that you will find this assignment to be much more challenging and difficult."

At least I agreed with him on that point, but not for the same reasons.

"This company is much bigger than your former company. We do things very well here and have spent years setting up the operations. We are very proud of what we have, the customers are happy, the board is happy, and the shareholders are happy. We don't want to mess that up.

"We view you as being young and inexperienced and are concerned about your wanting to change things here. Let me just be as clear as I can. I do not want you to change anything; I want you to keep a low profile for at least six months. If you see something that you believe needs changing, write it up and in six months we will talk about it. Is that clear?"

What was clear to me is that this guy might as well have locked me in a small cell somewhere in his cavernous office. Don't change anything . . . keep a low profile . . . I thought I was in an alternate universe. I had never heard of such a thing, especially for a guy who had been successful till then. I stuttered a bold, "Yes sir."

Let me save you the trouble of turning to the end of this chapter to see what happened. The general manager was transferred to the same location that I had just come from; that smaller, much simpler railroad. He was a dismal failure and was given early retirement.

It is one thing to drive change as a CEO; it is a different story when you are in the middle of the pack, and even worse when you are told not to change anything at all.

On the very day of the conversation with the general manager, I walked out of his office, much determined to drive results through continuous improvement, and I did. This book is about changing your work group, department, or company from within. You already have the desire, or you would have never picked up this book.

The Prize

One thing is for sure: whether individuals stick with the *status quo* or head into a maelstrom of creative destruction, the prizes for the winners are well worth having. For anybody with a desire to move up within an organization, there are essentially three ways (that I have observed in my nearly 30 years in business) to make it happen:

1. By being an effective change agent

2. By hitching your wagon to a rising star and hoping that when they advance, you will go with them

3. By doing nothing, laying low, and waiting for the phone to ring

The vast majority of senior leaders I talk to almost never complain about employees who act as change agents. They almost never get stressed out over people who stand up and fight for ideas, standards, and quality that they absolutely believe is in the best interest of the organization. However, whether it is on the golf course, in the board room, or over dinner, these same senior leaders will nearly always get their dander up when it comes to discussing employees who play it too safe, who never take a risk, and who are contributing to an aura of mediocrity.

In the early 1970s, while in college, Julia Stewart started her career as a waitress at an International House of Pancakes (IHOP). Julia loved being a server. She says, "I loved the fact that

I got feedback every day about how I was doing and what I could improve upon. I got very excited with the whole notion of serving people. Food service is a constantly changing and evolving business."[1]

After graduation, she began climbing the corporate ladder, beginning in marketing positions at Stuart Anderson's Black Angus & Cattle Restaurants, Spoons Grill & Bar, Burger King, and Carl's Jr. Julia then moved to Taco Bell, where she was the national vice president for franchise and license. In 2001, she returned to where it all started—IHOP—and she was named CEO in May 2002 when longtime chairman Richard Herzer retired.

A change agent throughout her entire career, Julia is constantly questioning what she and her organization are doing. Her first move as CEO was to spend three months visiting franchisees, vendors, corporate employees, and guests to hear from them what was working and what needed to be changed. Within a year, IHOP had registered the company's biggest increase in same-store sales in more than a decade.[2]

Change or Die!

Change is endemic in both our private and public lives. For organizations, the choice is stark: "Change—or die."[3] And yet, "Change: Few can do it, few can sustain it, few can survive it" seems to rule the day. At any moment in the business world, fully two-thirds of the Fortune 100—and probably an equally significant proportion of small and mid-sized companies as well—claim to be in the midst of some type of revamping or major change that is aimed at the behavior and skills of hundreds of thousands of people at all levels.

It is a worrying fact that annual research from the Harvard Business School reveals that only 30 percent of change initiatives at the Fortune 100 have ever produced an improvement in bottom-line results that exceeded the company's cost of capital, and only 50 percent led to an improvement in market share price. Not that these discouraging results were not for lack of trying. On average, each of the companies invested $1 billion in change programs over a 15-year period.[4]

These observations are dispiriting, but the alternatives to "not adjusting to change" are even bleaker. Failure to recognize increasingly powerful drivers of change—rapid technology development, growth in globalization of markets, rise of government regulation, reach of international terrorism, shift in market boundaries, ever-more demanding customers, and intensification of direct and indirect competition—has brought once-powerful industry icons to their knees. Digital, Prime, Wang, and Polaroid have sadly passed into history.[5] Others are just biding their time before the inevitable vanishing occurs. Indeed, their collective demise was felt to rest in an inability (or unwillingness) to adjust their culture—the way employees think and act—at least as much as shortcomings in shifting strategy, process, or structure.

If anything can be discerned, it is this: the future will not be like the past; the future will not be like we think; and most certainly, the rate of change will be faster than ever before.

Change and Growth

With stock markets and profits both edging up, corporate executives are daring to think again about the future. Emerging from their cost-cutting bunkers and shaking off the excesses of the turn-of-the-century boom, they are talking once more about strategies for growth. Admittedly, some companies like Kmart and US Airways are still wondering how to survive.

As they search for growth opportunities, however, companies face a classic dilemma, made more poignant by recent events: should they assume that the future will, more or less, be a continuation of the past; or should they try to anticipate the next big revolution? And, should they, essentially, hang on to what they've got (their "core competence"), or should they strike out for a brave new world?

After the dotcom disaster and much idle talk of a new economic paradigm, revolutions are distinctly out of favor. Belief in rapid change and dramatic responses has been shaken by the bursting of the stock market bubble and by the demise of such firms as Enron and WorldCom. There is now a widespread aversion to management fads. Most managers today are more interested in getting the basics right than in chasing the next rainbow.

In his book *Inevitable Surprises*, Peter Schwartz lists some of the future shocks that should not surprise us—the lengthening of the human lifespan, for example, where 60 becomes the equivalent of 40; the changing patterns of migration; the dominance of American economic and military might; and the existence of "a set of disorderly nations with the capacity to unleash terror, disease, and disruption" on the rest of the world. According to Mr. Schwartz, organizations that want to prepare themselves for these inevitable changes have a number of options. These include building effective intelligence systems, cultivating a sense of timing, and trying "to avoid denial." They also include putting in place mechanisms to engender creative destruction. "What processes, practices, and organizations have you actually dismantled in the last year or two?" asks Mr. Schwartz. "If the answer is none, perhaps it's time to get some practice in before urgency strikes."[6]

Change Agents

I believe, however, that nothing is more important in dealing with the "inevitable surprises" than having effective change agents in place. If change is inevitable, then it is necessary to adapt to it, or face the consequences. Nevertheless, even a cursory glance of books, articles, and other resources show that there is no common agreement on what "change" truly means, let alone "change agent." I have found that the word "change" has at least ten commonly used meanings:

1. change—having become different (undergo a change losing one's or its original nature—"She changed completely as she grew older"; "The weather changed last night")

2. alter, modify (cause to change; make different; cause a transformation—"The advent of the automobile may have altered the growth pattern of the city"; "The discussion has changed my thinking about the issue")

3. alter, vary (make or become different in some particular way, without permanently losing one's or its former characteristics or essence—"Her mood changes in accordance with the weather"; "The supermarket's selection of vegetables varies according to the season")

4. switch, shift (lay aside, abandon, or leave for another— "switch to a different brand of beer"; "She switched psychiatrists"; "The car changed lanes")

5. change clothes; put on different clothes ("Change before you go to the opera")

6. exchange, commute, convert (exchange or replace with another, usually of the same kind or category—"Could you convert my dollars into pounds?"; "He changed his name"; "convert centimeters into inches"; "convert holdings into shares")

7. exchange, interchange—(give to, and receive from, one another—"Would you change places with me?"; "We have been exchanging letters for a year")

8. transfer (change from one vehicle or transportation line to another—"She changed in Chicago on her way to the East coast")

9. deepen (become deeper in tone—"His voice began to change when he was 12 years old"; "Her voice deepened when she whispered the password")

10. remove or replace the coverings of ("Father had to learn how to change the baby"; "After each guest we changed the bed linens")

Using a non-scientific approach as I was preparing to write this book, I spent three separate days counting the number of times I used the word change during normal conversation. The first day I rang up 104 scores, the second 145, and the third a whopping 167. If you try it, you'll be surprised as well at the frequency of the use of the word.

Defining Change Agent

On account of the wide range of uses for the word "change," there is seemingly always some disagreement over the specific definition of a change agent. I view a change agent as a person who translates the strategic change vision of leaders into pragmatic change behavior. They will be the early adopters of the new values, actions, and skills required by the organization. Through this knowledge, they will act as a catalyst for the introduction of new ways of doing things across the four corners of the organization. Their goal will be to act as a positive virus infecting their host company.

This is not to say that a leader cannot be a change agent. Quite to the contrary. Individuals like Jack Welch while at GE, Herb Kelleher from Southwest, and the founders of Ben & Jerry's have created an infectious change-based environment within their organizations and across their industries. Nevertheless, the primary focus on this book will be on those great change agents—that every company must have—who never get mentioned in the *Wall Street Journal* or on CNBC, or at least until they become leaders themselves. As I will examine, it is these individuals that serve as critical intermediaries in creating an operational impetus for improved performance through changed behavior.

This book will look at the fundamental skill set that change agents need to become great. It will also describe how a change agent can acquire those proficiencies in order to successfully challenge existing norms of corporate behavior. Moreover, it will fully explore how the rewards of knowledge creation, learning, and innovation can be derived by the creation of great change agents from within an organization. If done the right way, the outcomes translate into sustained successes within the increasingly complex marketplace, where all organizations—big and small—have to interact and compete.

At its core, this book covers the ideas of successful people who believe in the salient skills the best change agents they have known possess. In my experience, these skills have always seemed to come back to one of five major themes. As I remember the great change agents I have encountered, most of them concentrated on a single, central principle. One alone would make a person noticeable and set them apart from their peers. The five of them together would define greatness.

Chapter 2

The Great
Change Mistakes

You can never solve a problem on the level
on which it was created.
Albert Einstein

IT SHOULD COME as no surprise that companies are full of people who have weathered the storm of change—people who have learned to live through change efforts without really ever having changed. Jeanie Duck wryly observes that change is intensely personal. And, for change to occur in any organization, each individual must think, feel, or do something different.[1] Much easier said than done.

A Brief Look at the Study of Change

Thirty years ago, if you wanted something changed as the leader of a traditional company, you simply spoke the words. The culture and belief system of the organization was more akin to a military structure, like the way railroads used to be run. The predictable behavior in that situation was compliance to the new business direction. For leaders in that organization, control was typically not questioned and employees understood what was expected of them. The values of control, consistency, and predictability created an environment where change was simply a plan to implement or an adjustment to a mechanical system.

More than a quarter of a century has passed. Organizational improvement initiatives—including W. Edwards Deming's teachings, post–World War II, the earliest quality circles from Toyota, Six Sigma from Motorola, Total Quality Management (TQM) from AT&T and Ford, empowered teams, and many others' initiatives—came to the forefront. Organizational leaders embraced, if at least for some period of time, one or more of these change initiatives.

Students of organizational improvement have been learning and practicing how to make changes to the operations of an organization as a mechanical system since Frederick Taylor's work on scientific management in the late nineteenth century. This mechanical system perspective focuses on observable, measurable organizational elements that can be changed or improved, including strategy, processes, systems, organizational structures, and job roles.

From this perspective, an organization is like a clock where each of the mechanical pieces can be changed or altered to produce a predictable and desirable solution. The change can be gradual, as seen in continuous process improvement methods such as TQM, or radical, as advocated in business process reengineering that began with the book *Reengineering the Corporation* by Michael Hammer and James Champy in the early 1990s.

Historically, organizations embracing this mechanical approach to business improvement typically did not embrace change-management concepts until their projects encountered resistance or faced serious problems during implementation. Even after this realization, many organizations' approach to change management was *ad hoc* and lacked a solid framework for actively managing change through the process. The tendency from an engineer's perspective was to isolate this "people" problem and then eliminate it or design a quick fix for this perceived obstacle to their improvement initiative.[2]

The other side of the story begins with psychologists. Concerned with how humans react to their environment, the field of psychology has often focused on how an individual thinks and behaves in a particular situation. Humans are often exposed to change, hence psychologists study how humans react to change. With his 1980 publication of *Transitions*, William Bridges became a predominant thinker in the field of human adaptation to change and his early text is frequently cited in organizational development books on change. However, only once or twice in this book does Bridges relate his theory to managing change in the workplace. It was not until later that Bridges began to write a significant body of work related to his theories of change and how they relate to workplace change management.

The net result of this evolution is that two schools of thought have emerged. Table 2.1 summarizes the key differences and contrasts the two approaches in terms of focus, practice, measures of success, and perspective on change.[3]

Observers of organizational changes in real life have realized that the extreme application of either of these two approaches, in isolation, will be unsuccessful. An exclusively "engineering" approach to business issues or opportunities results in effective solutions that are seldom adequately implemented, while an exclusively "psychology" approach results in a business receptive to new things without an appreciation or understanding for what must change for the business to succeed. Not all practitioners have traveled down these two extremes.[4]

Table 2.1
APPROACHES TO CHANGE

	Engineer	Psychologist
Focus	Processes, systems, structure	People
Practices	BPR, TQM, ISO 9000, Quality	Human resources, organizational development
Starting point	Business issues or opportunities	Personal change, employee resistance (or potential for resistance)
Measure of success	Organizational performance, financial and statistical metrics	Job satisfaction, turnover, productivity loss
Perspective on change	"Shoot the stragglers, bury the wounded."	"Help individuals make sense of what the change means to them."

A Look at Change Management

A few thought leaders in the change-management field were advocating a structured change-management process early on. Jeannine LaMarsh was actively using her organizational change model in the 1980s with companies like AT&T, Bell Laboratories, and later with Ford and Caterpillar. She authored the book *Changing the Way We Change* in 1995 and recently introduced the Managed Change process. In the book *Managing at the Speed of Change*, Daryl Conner begins with an emphasis on understanding the psychology of change and then moves to a structured change process. John Kotter, in *Leading Change*, presents an 8-step model for leading change initiatives. Contributions from both the engineering and psychology fields are producing a convergence of thought that is crucial for successful design and implementation of change.

In other words, an organization must constantly examine its performance, strategy, processes, and systems to understand what changes need to be made. Increasing external and internal factors have made this strategy essential for survival. However, an organization must also understand the implications of a new change on its employees, given their culture, values, history, and capacity for change. It is the front-line employees who ultimately execute on the new day-to-day activities and make the new processes and systems come to life in the business. As a direct result of these improvement strategies, a new way of thinking has evolved. It is founded on new values that include empowerment (make the right decision for the stakeholder), accountability (take ownership and pride in your work), and continuous improvement (look for ways to improve everything you do, every day). Today, we are much more likely to find organizations where a new generation of employees:[5]

- Take ownership and responsibility for their work

- Have pride in workmanship and look to improve their work processes

- Feel empowered to make decisions that improve their product and the level of customer service

So what is the problem? The evolution from the traditional values of control, predictability, and consistency—values that made change relatively simple to implement—to the new values focused on accountability, ownership, and empowerment have made the implementation of business change more difficult.

In his book *Stewardship*, Peter Block describes the traditional values that were the center pieces of traditional, patriarchal organizations: control, consistency, and predictability. These values dictated that decision making was at the top, leaving the execution and implementation to the middle and bottom layers of an organization.

In some cases of large-scale business process change in the early 1990s, the result was outright failure because business leaders had not shifted their actions to accommodate these new values. A leader in the old-value structure only had to issue the decree for change, and it happened. But when a leader tries this same approach today, employees shout back "Why?" "How does it impact me?" "If it isn't broken, why are you trying to fix it?"

In many ways, Block's advocacy for this shift has come true. Employees have been taught to question and analyze their day-to-day activities and are rewarded for doing so. There has been a real shift in the way people approach organizational change. The old, military style has been removed and a new, more dynamic approach has emerged.

Still, this creates a real dilemma. On the one hand, change is more difficult to implement if it comes from above because employees are more willing to speak up and resist. On the other hand, the more dynamic nature of present-day employees means that they are more willing to accept new ideas if they are good ones, regardless of where they come from. In other words, given the cultural shifts that have taken place over the past decades, all aspects of an organization—from the top to the bottom—are more prepared to deal with change than ever before.

Yet, as has been said before, that doesn't make it so. Such a difference between the theory and implementation of change makes Yogi Berra's dictum truer than ever: "In theory, there is no difference between practice and theory. In practice, there is."

The Great Change Mistakes

From my more than 25 years of experience in corporate America, I have observed that those who work in organizations that are charged with transforming them make five great mistakes when it comes to managing change. In the end, these mistakes, whether operating in unison or as separate factors, can squelch a movement toward change and can lead to the demise of the organization.

Mistake #1: Underestimating the Power of the Status Quo

The first common mistake is to overestimate the actual degree of contentment within the organization. Many managers I talk to are convinced that their people, customers, strategic alliance partners, or other stakeholders are generally satisfied with where the organization is. They constantly express their own satisfaction and seek out others who affirm their observations. They erroneously assume that affirmation expresses a greater desire to keep things moving in the same direction. Yet, they learn later that people were just being people and sharing their views in the moment or trying to make them happy. They misread the climate. And, as a result, they get hit hard when, seemingly out of nowhere, a push for change comes and no one is there to back them up.

For years at Procter & Gamble (P&G), the Pampers brand languished and struggled as the focus was almost exclusively on technology. Throughout most of the 1990s, the *status quo* in the company's baby division was on making ever-more leak-proof diapers. While arguably a worthwhile endeavor, the overreach on product design ultimately compromised the brand's relationship with the public and, as a result, sales fell year after year. Still, no one would challenge the *status quo*. That is until Deb Henretta came on board.

A self-described soccer mom and change agent who became president of P&G's global baby care division in 2003, Deb says her success is due to the fact that she is "constantly challenging the *status quo*."[6] She believes that battling the conventional wisdom of the day has helped her turn around Pampers, which led to new products and an increase of profits by more than 20 percent the first year under her watch.

For Deb, the first and most important step was "to get out of the factory, where the company was mired in the *status quo*, and back into the nursery again." For many years, research and development was focused on manufacturing process and operations, not on what was happening to the ever-changing market of baby care. This was the way it was done—until Deb broke out of the mold.

In nature, an object at rest will remain so unless a force greater than the force keeping it there causes it to move. This is true with the *status quo*. Until the tedious force of stagnation is overcome by a greater power, nothing will move and nothing will change. Often that greater power is friction.

Mistake #2: Favoring Consensus over Conflict

The second common mistake is the failure to recognize that conflict (friction) is a natural and necessary component to organizational growth and development. In today's often "touchy feely" world, conflict tends to be avoided at all costs. More and more, people would rather defer or run away from a potentially explosive situation than stay and fight, even if it is in the best interest of the organization.

A CEO acquaintance of mine at a regional hospital system was convinced that the highest-ranking physician was the most influential person in the organization. Everyone liked the doctor.

He was well respected and a nice person who always sought to build consensus. But the CEO mistook the universal appreciation for him to be an affirmation of his leadership. When the CEO began pushing for change, he was surprised to learn that the top physician had virtually no influence.

In fact, Susan, the chief administrator who worked in his department was the real power broker. She seldom said much and was thought by my CEO acquaintance to be someone who couldn't get along well with others. But, as he later learned, when an important decision was to be made, everyone would look to Susan for instruction. She would nod her opinion, and then others would speak. People would often disagree with Susan. Yet, because of her position, Susan knew everything that was going on, top to bottom. The CEO failed to notice that everyone looked to Susan for instruction. Susan gave her opinion with great subtlety, but gave it firmly for sure and did not hesitate to engage in conflict, whenever necessary.

At Tennessee Pride, makers of one of the nation's best-known sausages, consensus had been the dominant cultural characteristic of this family-owned business for decades. In fine Southern tradition, ill words were kept at bay and only those interested in ending their tenure with the company before retirement ever raised a voice in objection. In 1999, Larry Odom, the grandson of the company's founder, realized that success could dry up as fast as a water puddle blowing off steam under a hot summer sun. Odom observed at the time: "I knew if we didn't make a change, we'd end up being just the same. And that could be our end."[7]

The result was that James Stonehocker, an industrial engineer with no experience in meat manufacturing, was brought in to head up the firm's daily operations. "My technique walking in the door certainly had nothing to do with making sausage because people here already knew how to do that," Stonehocker emphasized. "I brought a different perspective on how we might reorganize ourselves to be more effective in that effort."

Stonehocker saw himself as a change agent. "Sure this company had fifty years of success, but will that take you into the future. No? Today's demands are different. Sometimes you have to break something apart and then put it back together." And that causes conflict.[8]

I remember from one of my executive education courses, the story of Alfred P. Sloan while he was running General Motors. When receiving unanimous support from his team for a particular project, the venerable leader would intentionally put the file folder on his credenza until it had gathered a sufficient amount of dust. His theory was that no idea could be that good. Sloan's notion was to let the project sit there for a while until someone could discover something wrong with it.

Mistake #3: Avoiding Risk, Rather Than Managing It

Risk is everywhere. It is all around us—in the bathtub, on the drive home, in our food. Risk is an uncertainty that affects our welfare, and is most often associated with loss or hardship. As risk is an inevitability to living our lives and there is no way we can get away from it, we try our best to manage it. We put rubber mats on the floor of the bathtub to get better traction. We wear seat belts to secure ourselves. We try to make sure that food is clean and properly cooked before we eat it. However, despite our efforts to manage risk, we still have to accept that it exists.

In all human endeavors, ascertained risk is managed risk. Generally speaking, when we establish the amount of risk in a given situation and implement ways to reduce the uncertainty surrounding it, we ultimately lower the level of risk associated with the event. Consequently, managing risk involves choosing among various alternatives to reduce the effects of risk.

Many Americans, however, have become experts in avoiding risk. They try to medicate, intoxicate, or litigate rather than deal with the inherent realities that come from living life. The ostrich with its head in the sand is how many people approach the risks they will inevitably face. Somehow, someway, they think they will not be affected.

Managing risk is *not* avoiding it. Instead, it involves finding the best available combination of risk and return, given the capacity to withstand the effects of inevitable risk.

An associate of mine was a senior manager at a mid-sized distribution company who was quite successful for almost ten years. Larry had a closet full of chips for quality efforts over many years. Although a "company man" through and through, he wanted to introduce a significant change in the design of his programs. Larry was convinced that this change would secure his firm's place (and his as well), while the industry was going through a tumultuous period. Larry was comfortable that he could pull it off pretty much by himself. After all, his years of success surely would give him that right.

However, as he began to evaluate the amount of risk he would be taking to execute the endeavor, he began to get cold feet. Larry did his own cost-benefit analysis and came to conclude that although the change was probably a necessary one, he might lose all of his credibility if things went bad. So, Larry avoided the risk of making a move toward change. Unfortunately, a year later, his company was purchased by a rival, and Larry was "reorganized" out of his job. At the meeting where he was "let go," Larry was told that although he had a fine record at the old company, he didn't exude the kind of risk-taking background the new company embodied.

John Chambers is recognized as one of the biggest risk takers in American business. Nevertheless, it hasn't always been that way. The celebrity CEO of Cisco Corp. learned firsthand the costs of avoiding risk when he was at Wang Laboratories in the early 1980s. Having started his career at IBM, Chambers became frustrated by the stifling bureaucracy at Big Blue. He left for greener pastures at Wang, which in 1980 looked ready to eat IBM's lunch. However, when the PC market began to develop, nobody at Wang, including Chambers, wanted to take the leap and get into this new, unknown area. Risk was avoided and the safe road was chosen. As Wang stumbled, Chambers had to lay off thousands of employees. Colleagues say it was a defining moment for Chambers, one that he never wanted to repeat.[9]

Mistake #4: Only Paying Lip Service to Creativity

It is both amusing and sad that many people whom I encounter tell me that their company asks them to explore their creative side, but the minute they come up with something that doesn't fit within the existing structure, it is squelched. In other words, they are told: try to be creative, but don't come up with new ways to change things either. Creativity is viewed more as a function, like regular department meetings, than an asset than can be leveraged.

A question I get all the time from my counterparts in other industries is: "Dave, what's the next big thing?" To be frank, I don't believe I'm the only person who is asked this question. I'm also certain it's not because of my ability to read the tea leaves that I am queried. It seems that those who constantly ask this question are hoping to extract someone else's creativity, when their own and their organization's is lacking.

I'm convinced that there is no "next big thing." There may be 10,000 "next big things." Maybe there's even a billion "next big things." Whatever the final number, they are leading to a new era. There's more opportunity to do things differently than ever before. Instead of focusing on any one big thing, I think it's better to focus on finding ways of adding value faster. And that takes an organizational dedication to creativity, not merely paying lip service to it.

Mistake #5: Failing to Encourage Change Agents

Being a change agent has always been a task left to those with a strong, if not well-coated stomach. This is due, at least in part, to the fact that for far too many organizations, except in a perceived crisis, the work of change agents is most often met with resistance. The resistance to change may come in four distinctly different time frames. The first will occur when the proposed change is first mentioned. Right away there is a reaction. The opportunity for change is blown off the map.

The second point occurs at the point of implementation. All the plans are made. The leadership has no hint there is going to be a reaction. There has been a little grumbling, but it hasn't been taken seriously. The organization is 24 hours from the proposed change, and all of a sudden there is an eruption of massive proportions. It catches the leadership by surprise.

An even larger surprise may occur about six months after the initial implementation. It appears that the change has been successfully implemented. All of a sudden there is a violent whiplash. Even the opponents of the change may be surprised by its intensity. Frequently, that reaction is sufficient to eliminate the change agent's ideas.

The fourth point is not as much of a surprise. That occurs when the change agent is removed—when the person who proposed and assisted with the implementation of the change leaves. And, as I have seen a number of times, at the meeting after a change agent left, the chair outlined an agenda to reverse most of the changes introduced by the departed person.

Those organizations that produce great change agents recognize these common mistakes and work to stay away from them. Their change agents develop a skill set that enables them to negotiate the perils of change as well as take advantage of the promises posed by it. The foundation of all of this is the development and unleashing of effective change agents throughout the organization, which ultimately leads to a more adaptable entity and one more likely to survive in turbulent times.

Chapter 3

The Change Agent Solution

Change has a considerable psychological impact on the human mind. To the fearful it is threatening because it means that things may get worse. To the hopeful it is encouraging because things may get better. To the confident it is inspiring because the challenge exists to make things better.
King Whitney Jr.

I WAS LEAVING a board meeting in Dallas a while back and found myself in an elevator with one of the board members. We had been discussing the happenings in the meeting that had to do with our organization making a radical change in our trademark. There had been a tremendous amount of opposition, mostly led by this same board member. In the end, after a very close vote, the board voted for the change. She was not happy.

"We in Texas have a saying, that if it ain't broke, don't fix it!" she said. There was not a lot I was going to say to that as I had already heard her side of the debate for the past two hours. I was thinking to myself that this whole "if it ain't broke" thing might apply to a fence in a cattle pasture, but it certainly did not apply to the business I was familiar with.

In years past we have seen books and articles titled, "If it ain't broke, then break it, and then fix it." After nearly 30 years in corporate America, I guess I just prefer the straight-forward approach that tries to improve the current state to a new level of performance.

This normally implies risk. But most people do not like to take risks. Why take a chance if you don't have to? What if it fails?

In my experience, people are much more worried about getting blamed than I am for getting the credit. So . . . if it ain't broke, don't fix it.

Several days after my "motivational session" with the general manager, I was out on an inspection trip in a major Western city where we had two rail facilities, one right downtown and another just on the edge of town. Our business was large enough only to keep both of the facilities running at half-capacity. When a facility runs at half-capacity, it becomes very difficult to gain a reasonable return on the assets base.

I thought to myself, we should close the facility downtown and move all of the operations to the other facility. This was doable; in fact it would provide tremendous efficiencies for the operation and improve customer service. The risk was that we would have little margin for error. Moreover, I was pushing the existing managers who were very comfortable with what they had. They did not see the need to change. It was a smooth operation that was never in trouble. The management was happy and the employees were happy. Why should they change?

The property in the downtown facility was prime real estate. We could not only make the operation more efficient, but could also sell the valuable land under it for a small fortune. However, what would happen if we closed the yard, consolidated the facilities, sold the expensive land, and operations ultimately suffered? There would be no back-up plan. It was all or nothing.

The only option was to manage the operation so that you did not need a failsafe. The problem was that this group had never done that before. It was like a high-wire act without a net. This change would result in the need for fewer employees. They were not going to like that one bit. There was no doubt that complaints would arise. They would probably reach the general manager's office 500 miles away very quickly.

At the tip of the sword, was the terminal manager, 20 years my senior. He was proud of his accomplishments. He planned to stay right there on that job until he retired. He did not want to do anything to jeopardize his plan. Life was good, he made his numbers, and no one bothered him. Why take a risk?

I had never taken on such a challenge with so many obstacles, barriers, and potential pitfalls. Yet, I could see very clearly the opportunity before me. I knew that it could work. I had almost everything figured right, except the terminal manager.

Not wanting to risk discussing the idea with him, I decided to bring in a study group of time and motion experts to quantify the work events at the facilities to demonstrate that the plan would work. The second day that these clipboard-laden efficiency eggheads showed up, the terminal manager called and asked me to fly out and meet with him. So I did.

"Dave, just level with me, I know that you are trying to prove something. Why don't you just tell me what you are thinking about," he said.

I thought carefully about what I was going to say before I said it. I then explained to him in very careful language what the experts and others thought. Matter of factly, he stated, "That's doable." It just about knocked me off my chair.

He added that they'd wanted to do this project for a long while, but had never received backing from senior management to pull it off.

Now they had the backing, and it was their idea, not mine. I was not changing anything, they were. I did not make the change, I facilitated it.

That was 20 years ago. We made the change. It worked. The property we sold to the city is now a major league sports stadium. We hit a home run and I learned a valuable lesson. While most people don't like change, they would rather be the changer than the changee. They like being the changer even more when they have support.

It wasn't until four years ago that I was able to sit in the stadium, enjoy a baseball game with a beer and a hot dog, and think about that whole sequence of events. I had a big smile on my face as I raised my glass in the air in a celebratory toast to the change agents who pulled it off.

People and Their Response to Change

People in an organization do not embrace change at the same time, or even at all. According to Everett Rogers' classic book *Diffusion of Innovation*, people adopt "innovations"—a.k.a. change—according to the various stages of a normal, bell-shaped curve (see Figure 3.1).

The "innovators" are the first 2.5 percent of the people in the organization to adopt an innovation. The next 13.5 percent to adopt the new idea are the "early adopters." The next 34 percent of the adopters are called the "early majority." The "late majority" are the next 34 percent to embrace the innovation, and the last 16 percent to adopt are called "laggards." It is very important that leaders, in bringing organizational change, focus their time and energy appropriately with each particular group of people.[1]

Innovators

These people have a great, almost obsessive, interest in new ideas. They desire the rash, the daring, and the risky. Their thirst

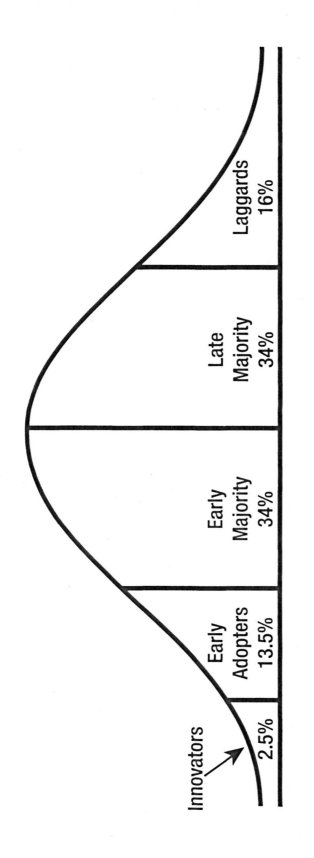

Figure 3.1
THE ADOPTION OF INNOVATION

for new ideas leads them to form networks beyond the confines of the local circles. They can cope with a high degree of uncertainty regarding the success of a new idea, and are willing to accept occasional setbacks. Many times, they will not bother to perfect the innovation, before moving on to the next one. Innovators may not be respected by the other members of the organization, but they are important to watch since they are frequently the gatekeepers in the flow of new ideas into the organization from outside its paradigmatic boundaries. Not surprising, these individuals are who we identify as change agents.

Early Adopters

These are the opinion leaders in the organization. The early adopters are the role models for others who respect them for their judicious "innovation-decisions." Potential adopters look up to them for advice and information about the change. They are not too far ahead of the other members of the organization, in contrast with the innovators who are seen as being too far out ahead. Early adopters decrease uncertainty about a new idea by adopting it, and then sharing their evaluation of the idea with their peers through personal relationships. This assists in bringing about organizational change. Early adopters can easily become change agents and add great value to the change process.

Early Majority

Comprising about one-third of the people, the early majority adopt new ideas just before the average member of the organization. They are not opinion leaders, but they do interact frequently with their peers. They make decisions slowly and carefully analyze the pros and cons of a new idea before adopting it. They follow with deliberate willingness in embracing change, but seldom lead. These are the critical supporters of a change initiative and change agents as the process evolves and moves through an organization. They can also become change agents, but clearly not at the same pace and intensity of the first two groups.

Late Majority

The late majority adopt innovations just after the average member of the organization. Skeptical and cautious, they do not adopt until most others have done so, and only then in response to the pressure of their peers and the new organizational norms. They are fence sitters, who, if they sense the change agents are going to succeed, will get on the bandwagon.

Laggards

The last in the organization to embrace change, laggards possess almost no opinion leadership. Typically, they are somewhat isolated in their relationship networks, interacting primarily with others who have relatively traditional values. They usually make decisions in terms of what has been done previously, and are typically suspicious of change and change agents.

Nearly all great change agents will come from the first two groups—innovators and early adopters. Not surprising, almost every leader of every organization I know of falls within one of those two categories. In other words, those people who move up and become leaders are most likely change agents themselves.

Manuel Gonzalez is a tiger. At least, that's what his employers at Baja Fresh Mexican Grill call him. "He's one of our tigers. He's definitely one of our outstanding general managers," says Steve Heeley, senior vice president of operations for the company. In the lingo of the Thousand Oaks, California–based chain, being called a tiger is a compliment. A tiger is someone who is alert, takes initiative, and acts decisively as a change agent. And Gonzalez's sales results show that to be the case.

In 2001, Gonzalez won "Turnaround Restaurant of the Year" at his Simi Valley, California, location. Since he was named manager in June 2000, the unit has posted strong sales increases. Between 2000 and 2001, sales increased between 12 percent and 15 percent, Gonzalez says. In 2003 sales grew between 5 percent and 8 percent. "That restaurant was definitely heading in the wrong direction before Manuel took over," says Tom Bryan, regional operator of Baja Fresh and direct supervisor of Gonzalez's restaurant.

According to Bryan, Gonzalez has achieved more than sales gains; he also has mastered the art of customer service and achieved strong financial results. "He's got all three points of the triangle," Bryan says. "He's done a great job." For Gonzalez, running a great operation for Baja Fresh is a passion. "What you put in is what you get out of Baja Fresh," Gonzalez says. One of the things the company gives, according to Gonzalez, is career advancement.

When Gonzalez started at the chain four years ago, he was hired as an assistant manager. Soon he was promoted to general manager at the Simi Valley restaurant. His goal is to be a district operator. Gonzalez tries to encourage other people to move up the ranks at Baja Fresh. He believes that such encouragement is a form of motivation.

Gonzalez is glad he pounced on the opportunity to work at Baja Fresh when he did. He graduated from Van Nuys High School, in the Los Angeles Unified School District. His first job was as a cook at a family-owned restaurant. He moved up to shift manager and then general manager. He was opening a restaurant for the chain in Simi Valley when a recruiter from Baja Fresh asked him if he wanted to make a change. At first Gonzalez did not pay attention. When the person came back the following week, Gonzalez decided to have lunch with him and find out about Baja Fresh. He then talked to employees of the company to find out if they liked it. One of the people he talked to was a cashier who was in the process of becoming a general manager. That told him that the company promotes from within and values people who make change their number one priority. He liked that.

After a few interviews, including one with Steve Heeley, vice president of operations, he was in the company. "Four years later I'm glad I made this change," he says. Today, he works five days a week for a total of 50 to 55 hours. He closes the store one day a week and has Wednesdays and Sundays off. In Gonzalez's eyes there is always room for change and improvement.[2]

The Long View of Change Agents

The recognition of the importance of change agents is not a recent phenomenon. In fact, two of my most favorite change agents lived centuries ago. One of them was critical in the creation of the Christian faith. The other was one of the founders of modern science.

In any list of the apostles, most people begin by naming the "Big Three": Peter, James, and John. The remainder list might mention Matthew, and Judas of course, and "doubting" Thomas, and . . . let's see . . . who were the rest anyway? Most know little or anything about Andrew—except that he was Peter's brother and one of the apostles.[3]

But of all the apostles, none is probably more common to the people we meet every day—and maybe even to ourselves—as Andrew. He is the man who sits next to you on the airplane, drives the truck, waits on you in a store, sits at the desk next to yours, or delivers your pizza. Andrew is all around you. You meet him every day, and he holds the key to many situations.

There is something significant in the fact that Andrew was the first of Jesus' apostles to be called. Andrew has been usually referred to as Simon Peter's brother. He himself was not a leader of men. Andrew was not aggressive like his brother. Nor was he a great speaker or visionary. Yet it was Andrew who took the chance and introduced Jesus to Simon. And, because of that introduction, the rock on which Jesus would build his church came onto the scene.

It is all very well to be impressed with the contributions that are made by the great women and men—the people who seemingly do everything well—and who usually get the notice, publicity, praise, and rewards.[4] However, what we are all inclined to forget is the fact that behind those folks are the unnumbered hosts of ordinary men and women whose names are never printed, but whose quiet unassuming work makes the successes of the leaders possible. We also find Andrew as the one who took the initiative and gathered up the loaves and fishes for Jesus when the 5,000 were fed.

The vast majority of people fall into the two-talent class—the men and women who are taken for granted but without whom success could never be accomplished. They have a job to do, and they are willing to do it without complaint. These people always have—and continue—to make up the biggest group of change agents.

Isaac Newton was widely quoted in his day as saying that he had seen farther by standing on the shoulders of giants. But he did not believe it. As James Gleick aptly writes about Newton, "He was born into a world of darkness, obscurity, and magic; led a strangely pure and obsessive life, lacking parents, lovers and friends; quarreled bitterly with great men who crossed his path; veered at least once to the brink of madness; cloaked his work in secrecy; and yet discovered more of the essential core of human knowledge than anyone before or after."[5]

Newton viewed everything around him differently. He was a change agent in the purest sense of the term. He constantly questioned everything. He was the chief architect of the modern world. He answered the ancient philosophical riddles of light and motion, and he effectively discovered gravity. He showed how to predict the courses of heavenly bodies and so established the place of human beings in the cosmos. He made knowledge a thing of substance: quantitative and exact. He established principles, and they are called his laws.[6]

Successful Change Agents and Their Efforts

Managers who initiate activities-centered programs, like 7-step problem solving, statistical process control, and total quality management training, falsely assume that one day results will magically materialize. They recognize that because there is no explicit connection between action and outcome, improvements seldom come to fruition. Robert Schaffer and Harvey Thomson hit it on the head when they state, "The performance improvement efforts of many companies have as much an impact on operational and financial results as a ceremonial rain dance on the weather. While some companies constantly improve measurable performance, in many others, managers continue to dance round the campfire—exuding faith and dissipating energy.[7]

Constant and inevitable change is something that cannot be pushed aside because it is too hard, costly, or time consuming. Because organizations of all sizes are immersed in a virtual cyclone of change, they cannot sit idly by and do nothing. Unfortunately, many initiatives to deal with the change fail. And while failure due to resistance, poor implementation and follow-through, or a lack of an imagination, may constitute some of the reasons change initiatives don't succeed, I am convinced the majority of failures are due to a shortage of great change agents within the organization.

When Brenda Barnes left her $2-million-a-year post at PepsiCo. in January 1988, her departure helped spark a national debate about the pressures modern women face in balancing home and careers. She famously told one popular talk show host that she no longer wanted to miss "another of my kids' birthdays." Now that her children are grown, Brenda Barnes has not only reentered corporate life but was also recently named chief executive of Sara Lee Corp.

After leaving Pepsi, Barnes did manage to keep in touch with the corporate world. She remained on several boards, including the New York Times Co., Sears Roebuck & Co., and Lucas Films, Ltd., the company controlled by Star Wars director George Lucas. "I think I gained a lot of experience from each of those companies," said Barnes. "I had different vantage points of different industries, with different challenges, different transformation plans, and different workplace issues. You learn a lot when you see it from different companies."

"I think it's the challenge she faces at Sara Lee, and it's a considerable challenge, that has probably attracted her to the company," said Walter Scott, Professor of Management at the Kellogg School. "Many of us are driven by the chance to transform and really make a difference." Scott met Barnes several years ago when she was an adjunct professor at Kellogg and coming to grips with lecturing students. "She's very humble and does not appear to have much of an ego," said Scott. "She has a way of letting everyone participate in the process."

Barnes, who has a reputation for embracing change, says she believes that communications are key to success in business. "I really believe that clarity of direction is critical," said Barnes. "I believe in treating people with respect and giving them the freedom to do their job is essential."[8]

Change agents are result-oriented folks who viscerally understand that any payoffs from the infusion of more and more activities are marginal at best.

They are the ones who avoid the mistakes elaborated in the last chapter and, instead, challenge the *status quo*, embrace conflict, manage risk, stoke the fire of creativity, and bring along new change agents with them. The next five chapters will illustrate the outcomes that effective—and, ultimately, great!—change agents embody.

Chapter 4

Great Change Agents Challenge the Status Quo

Conviction is worthless unless it is converted into conduct.
Thomas Carlyle

IT IS EASIER to make changes when you are the "new guy." If you are not the new guy, look for ways to make it appear you are new. Just after I joined the Santa Fe Railway in 1993, I was engaged in a conversation with one of the vice presidents of the company. He was asking me how everything was going on and if there was anything he could do to help me. I replied that I was looking forward to working past being new and becoming a member of the "club." I still remember his response as though it was yesterday. "Keep being the new guy as long as you can," he said. "Make that your goal instead of being a member of the club."

He went on to say that new managers are expected to make changes, that their whispers are perceived as shouts. "People watch their every move; they wait with anticipation of everything they are going to say," he remarked. "People are primed for change when there is a new guy, don't disappoint them." And, he was right.

As I think back now on that scene with the general manager ten years earlier, his telling me to keep a low profile and not to change anything was a sure recipe to keep me neutralized for a long time. It is one thing to have your boss do that to you, but it is another to impose that on yourself. Don't be guilty of that mistake.

I have seen several circumstances where a new CEO comes into a company and changes a policy or an established institution of the company to make the point that change is coming and everyone had better be ready.

In the days before the prevalence of "business casual," I saw one CEO make Fridays not just casual dress day, but western dress day, complete with jeans and boots. His point was that the previous culture was too formal and stuffy, and that people needed to "loosen up."

Another CEO decided just after coming on board that he was closing the executive dining room and making it a cafeteria for all employees to use—his point being that the "elitism" of the former CEO was stifling to the type of teamwork and camaraderie he was expecting from the organization. Similar changes include eliminating assigned parking spaces and other perks that go with the top brass. They are all examples that demonstrate that the new leader is actually doing something, rather than just keeping the seat warm, and that change will be part of the *status quo*.

Beyond that, and even more effectively, they terminate a high-ranking member of the "old guard"—usually an executive or senior vice president who is clearly seen as a "fixture" in the company and an icon for everything that reflects the *status quo*. Believe me, this gets everyone's attention. This clearly establishes who is in charge, and that change is going to be part of the new culture. Driving out these sacred cows sets the stage for what is going to come.

Then, they truly set the "vision." It is much easier when you are new to set the course for change. The great ones show specifically, in quantifiable terms, what exactly the goals and vision are for the group. Usually, these are departures from the previous regime. If the old strategy was market share growth, the new strategy will be customer retention and organic growth. After all, what CEO comes in and says, "I am going to do my best to keep it rolling just like good old Bob," or even better, "I will do my best not to screw up what Bob has already set up." Most new guys count the seconds it takes for their predecessor to say their good-byes at the going away/retirement party and for the office to be cleaned out. Move-in time means change time, and time is a-wasting when you are new.

I was spending some time with one of our middle managers in a formal mentoring program two years ago when I brought up the subject about what changes had been made since they took over. They replied that they had not made any changes because when they took over, the employees met the new manager at the doorstep and begged to just let things settle down (as Bob, the predecessor, had made so many radical changes to the operation). The new manager relented and said okay, no changes.

We talked for a while about the "new guy" advantage to make change and I inquired as to how long the managers had already been there. With reservation in their voice, they responded that they had been on the job 18 months, and had done little to change things. I tried to reassure the manager that while they had missed a major opportunity, all was not lost. They would just have to create a perception that these were new times that they all must react to and that it was crucial that changes be made. Whether it is a critical event, like losing a big account, a major accident, or a significant external issue like a new competitor or a change in laws or regulations . . . make it appear that things are "new."

John Kotter, in his book *Leading Change*, refers to it as "Cre-

ate a Sense of Urgency." This puts the manager back in the lime-
light or fishbowl, makes the whispers appear like shouts, and sets
the bias for change.

After our discussion, the managers decided right then, that
they were going to immediately set a course to establishing a reason for the need for change. It worked, and things at that location are much better.

Staying New

Change is rarely easy for one person to make happen, especially if they've been around for a while. This is why being new
and *staying new* is a formidable task, to say the least. However,
far too many people come on board and believe they shouldn't
make waves and maintain the *status quo* until they get settled.
For frontline managers, simple things like moving the location
of the time clock or reorganizing the break room sets the tone
that change is coming and to be ready.

To stay new in the face of the *status quo* and be able to launch
a successful challenge against it, I find that effective change agents
are able to maintain their good intentions and perform actions
that keep people guessing what they are going to do next. Doing
so keeps them wondering: "My goodness, what are they are going
to do next?" It keeps the environment in which the change agent
operates fresh, and provides a place from which to attack the
status quo.

Why Integrity Is Critical to "Staying New"

Underpinning the endeavor to stay new is the integrity of the
change agent. This **must** be driven by the desire to do the right
thing for the right reasons. In our first book *Defining the Really
Great Boss*, I spent a lot of time detailing how critical integrity is

for the great leader. The same is equally true for the change agent. While it is not my intention to restate what we wrote previously, some attention to this vital topic is needed to help elucidate the importance of character for great change agents.

Doing the right thing for the right reasons is founded on the pillars of consistency, reputation, and accountability. These factors, more than any other, serve as the inputs of doing the right thing. They drive the intentions and actions of the change agent. When directed in the proper manner, they inevitably lead to a right outcome, at the right time, at the right place, and in the right way.

Bulletproofed Consistency

The Latin root of the word integrity is similar to that of integer, meaning whole number. The concept of wholeness, or consistency, is clearly relevant. For now, we shall take *behavior and decisions that are consistently in line with our principles* as our working definition of acting with integrity. One of the important elements of integrity is consistency—if we are unpredictable and if our decisions are dependent upon the day of the week and the way we are feeling, others are unlikely to see us as maintaining integrity.

After several different positions over the first five years of my career, I found myself in charge of a large divisional operation in Little Rock, Arkansas. This was in the early 1980s before the days of many of the buzzwords that exist today to describe management-types. I got things done. I made decisions. However, what I did was, for the most part, based on pre-established guidelines emanating from policies, operating rules, and instructions. In reality, I was more of an administrator of set policies— a.k.a the *status quo*—than an actual decision-maker.

I worried a lot about consistency. I battled every day with

thoughts like "If I allow this exception, it will weaken my power"; "If I do it for one, I will have to do it for everyone"; and "I must be consistent, and that means doing it by the book and not challenging the status quo."

One night, I was in the office working late. Most of the staff had gone home. There was a knock at the door and two employees asked if they could come in. They were two burly seasoned railroad workers who sat down on the edge of their seats. Although I don't recall what they asked me, I've always remembered how the conversation started out. The first began by saying, "Mr. Dealy, we came here tonight to ask you to listen to us about a problem we have. We know that most supervisors would say that our company has a policy for this and it clearly defines what we must do." Then the second one took over saying, "in this case, the policy is very clear on how our situation should be handled. In fact, if it were anyone other than you, we would have given up long ago, but we believe that our situation is a little bit different and deserves special consideration."

What they said after that still sticks with me as though it was yesterday. "We have been watching what you do and how you do it. We have always believed that you would always do the right thing for the right reasons. So we are asking you to do . . ."

That was a defining moment in my life. I thought, they were watching me? They trusted me? They believed that I would do the right thing for the right reasons? What should I do?

As it unfolded, I don't even remember if I granted their request, whatever it was. I do remember, however, having the unquestionable and unconditional feeling that they trusted me and they would continue to trust me, regardless of the outcome of my decision. I was in awe of that situation and their trust. From that point on in my career, I was determined to examine what it was that I did to earn their trust and respect and how to make change happen in ways that continued to develop that type of credibility.

After 26 years in business, for even the best of rules, instructions, and policies, I have found there are always exceptional situations that lie outside their original intent. Dishearteningly, however, I have seen many a manager forcing these situations into a box like a square peg in a round hole. They work hard to make it either black or white because then the decision is easy—and it conforms within the parameters of the *status quo*. But, forcing things to be black or white does not build credibility. Recognizing when they are gray and reacting accordingly does.

Rob Krebs, chairman, CEO, and president of the Santa Fe Railway and then the BNSF Railway, a man who I have had the pleasure of working for since 1993, always says, "Consistency is the hob-gob of the simple mind."

Built Reputations

Many suppose that their organization's hard assets like machinery, inventory, or technology give them the ultimate edge over their competitors. Others say it is their firm's vast financial resources that keep them on top. Although each of these is critical to an organization's ultimate success, its reputation is the most important asset. People buy your products and services, sell you theirs, and seek to develop relationships with you based primarily upon how they perceive your organization. Your reputation provides the foundation to that perception. To be blunt, you must do everything you can to preserve and enhance the reputation your company has with its customers, suppliers, strategic alliance partners, employees, and the public at large.

Change agents realize that theirs and the organization's meaningful and valuable reputation begins with one fundamental factor: choices. The degree of success of a change agent will be dramatically shaped by the strength of their commitment to doing the right thing all the time. Everyday change agents are confronted with myriad choices facing them. Some of the options will be the correct choice, others won't be. By making the right choices, the change agent and the organization will receive the payoffs associated with reputations of honesty, integrity, quality, and caring in everything they do. Make the wrong choices and the change agent and the organization will be plagued with mistakes, ongoing problems, unavoidable disasters, irreparable damage to their reputation, and quite possibly, even their ultimate demise.

Perhaps the real tragedy of poor choice is the mental anguish, pain, and constant scrutiny that emerge from a ruined reputation. The origin of the word "reputation" comes from the Latin word *reputatio*, which means reckoning. Reputation, at its core, can be defined as all that is generally believed about one's character, respectability, credit, integrity, or notoriety. Reputation is what the bosses' image, performance history, and track record means in people's minds.

A good reputation is the building and sustaining of a boss' name. Henry Ford said it right when he observed, "You can't build a reputation on what you are going to do." By paying attention to what you are doing, you'll be able to construct and maintain a strong perception of yourself and your organization.

Real Accountability

Many people don't even know what accountability means. To give you an answer using Webster's dictionary, the word "accountability" means "an obligation or willingness to accept responsibility or to account for one's actions." At its core, accountability is really the responsibility to act. However, confusing accountability with responsibility obscures the obligation to act.

At the end of the day, it is critical to understand that people account, not intangible things like "corporations" and "governments." For bosses, reciprocal accountability is the obligation of people in senior posts in organizations to answer to members of the organizations for what they intend and what they contribute.

For every important responsibility, there is accountability. Accountability is the obligation to answer for the discharge of responsibilities that affect others in important ways. The answering is for intentions as well as results. Whenever a boss has an important responsibility, he or she has an obligation to answer to stakeholders for their decisions.

Change agents have, for quite some time, been held accountable for results. In most businesses, people live and die by the numbers on their scorecard. For many of these numbers, there are trade-offs that have to or should be made for the good and betterment of the change agent's own department or the good of the company. I have seen many change agents deal away their credibility because they manage to their numbers at all cost, even when it is obvious that the decision is detrimental to the greater good.

I have had people publicly state that they know the right thing to do is X but state that they're going to do Y because of their "numbers." They are worried about themselves and what others will think—nothing else. They are obviously not worried about those around them who can see this very clearly. How can they respect this individual? They really can't.

Intentions and Staying New

Rooted in the mindset of doing the right things for the right reasons, the intentions of the great change agent are characterized as:

- Unsullied

- Unmarked

- Unblemished

This provides the change agent with the moral high ground. This will not protect them from criticism or attack. However, it will render useless any argument made against them that their attempts to challenge the *status quo* are anything but well meaning. Time and time again, I have seen firsthand budding change agents who lose the ability to impact the organization because their motives are questionable and purely self-serving.

This isn't to say, however, that self benefits are a bad thing when it comes to trying to change things. Quite to the contrary. Instead, what loses credibility—and ultimately effectiveness—for the change agent is when the best interests of the organization are pushed aside in favor of their personal gain. Such an unfolding compromises the change agent and all their efforts.

Chapter 5

Great Change Agents Embrace the Necessity of Conflict

Change means movement. Movement means friction. Only in the frictionless vacuum of a nonexistent abstract world can movement or change occur without that abrasive friction of conflict.
Saul Alinsky

WHILE I WAS growing up, my mom would always say, "Eat your vegetables first, they are good for you." I didn't like them then, and I still don't, but she was right. There are some things in life that we don't like, but they are still good for us. I personally don't wake up in the morning thinking, "I can't wait to have a big bowl of conflict for breakfast." Actually, I don't know anyone whose elevator goes all the way to the top who does. No one likes conflict. Yet every change agent is faced with it on a regular basis. Some face minimal conflict, others face horrific conflict, but none escape.

Challenging the *status quo* will inherently lead to conflict. There is no doubt about it. Some people will fight a move to change things because it threatens their existence within the organization. Others will view such actions as power plays meant to advance the interests of the change agent. Still others will disagree with the direction in which the changes are taking the organization.

Unfortunately, many businesses focus on process change, often overlooking people change. Change is about aligning people, resources, and culture with a shift in organizational direction. Many such shifts result in a major makeover of the organization and/or its component systems. In today's business environment, such radical changes are often initiated by critical events, such as an appointment of a new CEO, new ownership brought about by a merger or acquisition, deregulation or market moves in an industry, or a dramatic failure in operating results.

Radical change used to occur infrequently in the life cycle of an organization. However, in a knowledge-based and technology-driven economy, the frequency of change has increased tremendously. And, as a result, conflicts inevitably arise.

An even more common form of organizational change is incremental change, or frame-bending change. This is change that occurs more frequently as part of an organization's natural evolution and with less dramatic impact. Typical changes of this type would include new products, new technologies, and new systems being introduced and implemented. Although the nature of the organization remains relatively the same, incremental change builds on the existing ways of operating and seeks to enhance them. Nevertheless, conflicts will take place.

As discussed, the success of organizational change depends largely on change agents who facilitate and support the change process. A change agent is a person who takes responsibility for changing the existing pattern of behavior of another person or social system. Change agents must be alert to situations or people needing change, open to good ideas, and able to support the implementation of new ideas into actual work processes. They must also embrace the inevitable nature of conflict.

You Can't Hide From Conflict

A British friend of mine once told me of a story in the early 1980s of a retired couple who were so alarmed by the threat of nuclear war that they undertook a serious study of all the inhabited places on the globe. Their goal was to determine where in the world would be the least likely place affected by a nuclear war—a place of ultimate peace and security. They studied and traveled, traveled and studied. Finally they found the place. And on Christmas they sent a friend a card from their new home—in the Falkland Islands. However, their "paradise" was soon turned into a war zone by Great Britain and Argentina in the conflict now recorded in history books as the Falklands War.

The civil rights activist James Baldwin is credited with observing, "Most of us are about as eager to be changed as we were to be born, and go through our changes in a similar state of shock." The proactive nature of change agents almost guarantees that a state of perpetual conflict will exist.

One of my favorite analogies on the subject of change and its inevitability comes from management consultant Peter Vaill. He points out that society is rapidly changing and compares this to living permanently in white water. You have two choices: either jump out of the canoe or grab a paddle. If you have ever rafted, you know that steering a course through white water is not an easy task. Nor is living with constant change. Vaill observes that navigating the rapids is hard work: things are only partially under control, yet the effective navigator of the rapids is not behaving randomly or aimlessly. Intelligence, experience, and skill are being exercised, albeit in ways that we hardly know how to perceive, let alone describe. If you understand that responses to change are normal and predictable—and that conflict is predictable—then chances are that change can be managed.[1]

Studies have shown that the most common reaction to change

is resistance. I am sure you have experienced this. The reasons why people resist change are many. Chief among them are excessive uncertainty. If we don't know where the next step will lead, we tend to stay put. Our desire for familiar surroundings (or processes) is strong. Change can also cause us to question our competence to continue to do our job or to fear others questioning how we have done that job in the past. Finally, resistance is fueled by the specter of losing control. This is all very natural . . .

The Misconceptions Surrounding Conflict

Our attitude toward conflict shapes how we as leaders handle conflict. What is your initial attitude toward conflict? Is it dread? Denial? Maybe fear? Perhaps, "What a hassle!" How about procrastination or deflection? ("Let someone else handle it.") Or do you accept conflict as a natural part of life, not preferred, but part of the reality of leadership and choose to use it as a tool for growth and progress? The last response is the wise and healthy response, but also the most difficult.

Misconceptions about conflict do change agents a disservice when it comes to seeing the value in conflict and attaining resolution. One misconception is that all conflict is negative. There are many forms of conflict from Supreme Court issues to scientific debate to methods of child rearing between loving parents that sharpen all of us and develop us as people. Admittedly, there is a difference between disagreement and conflict. It is, however, a fine line and something as subjective as an individual's personality may cause one person to view a situation as a simple disagreement and another to view the same situation as conflict.

Whichever end of the spectrum you are at, and whether or not you perceive it as negative or positive, strongly shapes how you handle it. If you perceive it as negative, you may attempt to do anything to avoid it or get out of it as soon as possible. If you see it as positive, not enjoying it, but embracing the potential for growth, you will have a completely different approach and outcome. Another misconception is that people are always hurt by conflict. That is not true. It is similar to going to the dentist. I find no joy whatsoever in going to my dentist, but the long-term results are positive and in my best interest. One of the things I thoroughly enjoy is deep political discussion. Not that I'm wise or profound, actually more the opposite, but I am a good student and I love to learn. Tension can mount quickly over political convictions, but as a result of some of the most difficult conversations, I have learned the most. If I had beefed up my defenses, stopped listening, and launched an attack, I may have felt victorious, but I would have learned nothing.

A third misconception is that people are too fragile to handle conflict. Someone once said, "Without conflict, there would be no free market." The business world is packed with conflict and it is something all change agents must manage.

Derivatives of Conflict

Conflict has tenable benefits for change agents if they look for them:

Conflict Helps Discover the Real You and the Strength of Your Character

Most of us will never be tested in a dramatic way like the Old Testament character Job. But life has its way of testing us in everyday ways as well. How do you react when someone cuts you off while driving? What about when you receive an angry e-mail from someone? Or a telemarketing call in the middle of dinner? Your response reveals much about the real you. How little or how much it takes to upset you gives great insights to your character. How quickly you pursue positive solutions and forgiveness and how slow you are to anger tells a significant story. We have much to learn from conflict.

Conflict Often Serves as the Crucible of a New and Better Way

Some time back, Peter Jennings narrated an ABC special titled *The Century: America's Time.* The documentary did an excellent job portraying our country's story over a 100-year span of time, hitting the joys and sorrows, victories and defeats. One scene sticks with me of a World War I veteran's personal story. Sitting in his chair, the old man said with great passion, "Nobody wins in a war. The Germans lost, but we didn't win. There must be a better way." This man saw, from the front lines, one of history's ugliest wars in which 9 million lives were lost. And his response was to say that there must be a better way. Conflict forces us to explore a better way. When we do, life is better. When we don't, history repeats itself. Very few things of great value come without a price.

As John Dewey observed, "Conflict is the gadfly of thought. It stirs us to observation and memory. It instigates to invention. It shocks us out of sheep like passivity, and sets us at noting and contributing."

Conflict Helps You Discover Who Your Friends Are

Conflict is inevitable, but combat is optional. Conflict will quickly let you know who you can count on and who will be by your side when the going gets tough. Few things are more valuable than knowing who you can trust. Take a moment now and make a list of those people who are on your side and share your interests.

To paraphrase Robert Townsend, a great change agent doesn't try to eliminate conflict; he tries to keep it from wasting the energies of those around him. If people fight you openly when they think that you are wrong, that's healthy. And that can let you know who your friends are.[2]

Listen to the Naysayers

Out of constant conflict and resistance, however, often arises a degree of callousness on the part of the change agent. The result is that change agents "damn the torpedoes" and tune out to those around them. They quit listening after they've heard "We can't do that" or "It's been tried before" over and over.

Change agents may even tend to discount and marginalize the opinions of the naysayers to their own detriment. A great change agent will recognize, even if it is hard for their ego to accept, that even the words of the "doom and gloomers" have some value. That is why great change agents embrace the conflict, rather than run and hide from it.

Carly Fiorina, the former chairman of Hewlett-Packard (HP), was driven to change HP and transform it. Her chosen strategy was to execute a controversial merger with Compaq, a Texas firm a world apart culturally from HP's Silicon Valley ways. From the beginning, however, things appeared frayed as Ms. Fiorina apparently resisted suggestions that she hire a chief operating officer who could have helped her to cope with the details of the merger—including the inevitable conflicts that would arise.

Things got even more difficult when later on as Ms. Fiorina seemingly focused more and more of her energies on defending the merger rather than listening to the critics, who were offering some viable options. Her tough, "damn the torpedoes" style clashed with the collegial culture that HP's staff were used to and many key managers ultimately left the company, further weakening the organization. By failing to embrace conflicts and the benefits that can be extracted from it, Ms. Fiorina put herself in a position that ultimately compromised her ability to be an effective agent of change.

Chapter 6

Great Change Agents Manage Risk, Not Avoid It

In a time of drastic change it is the learners who inherit the future. The learned usually find themselves equipped to live in a world that no longer exists.
Eric Hoffer

IT IS AN often unspoken truth that change comes from dissatisfaction. Dissatisfaction with the direction of the organization. Dissatisfaction with the leadership, the vision, the environment, or any number of other things. The great change agent assesses the chances for change by evaluating the level of dissatisfaction within the group. If dissatisfaction is strong, the potential for change should exist. Conversely, if dissatisfaction is low, the potential for change would seemingly be difficult to achieve.

However, to be effective, a great change agent must also deliberately develop dissatisfaction where it doesn't exist. Just because people cannot see something that needs to be changed doesn't mean that it shouldn't be altered. In cases where change is critical to the organization's well being, seeking to create the right level of dissatisfaction becomes a mandate for the great change agent.

Picking the Right Battles

It is at this point in the study of the great change agent that I come to the critical issue of risk. A move toward creating dissatisfaction is an inherently risky venture. The last thing anyone wants to hear when they are content is that things are not good.

Those who best impact their organizations have learned to pick their battles carefully, and possess the courage to do so. With their boss, co-workers, strategic alliance partners, strangers in the checkout line, there are times when it's better just to let some things pass. You have only so many chips of credibility or influence to play. The great change agent recognizes this before choosing to take a stand and fight; they are sure the issue really matters. But such an approach to determining what is important and what is not is foreboding.

Managing risk is *not* avoiding it. Instead, it involves finding the best available combination of risk and return, given the capacity to withstand the effects of risk. Effective risk management involves anticipating outcomes as well as planning strategy and tactics in advance, given their likelihood, not merely reacting to those events after they occur. At its core, managing risk is proactive.

The key to managing risk and determining the important battles to fight is found in assessing the amount of potential damage posed by a particular activity, behavior, or individual. Great change agents tend to pair and rank the highest risk threats with the highest risk vulnerabilities that are most likely to occur. Then, they rank the marginal risk threats with the marginal risk vulnerabilities. And finally, the low risk threats with low risk vulnerabilities. This enables the great change agent to allocate their resources in such a way that it leads them to better manage risk and ultimately better impact the organization. Typically, the probability levels of an undesired event are paired with the severity levels of that same event. Table 6.1 illustrates how probabil-

Table 6.1
RISK PROBABILITY AND SEVERITY LEVELS

Probability Levels of Something That Should Be Changed[1]

Probability Level	Specific Event
A Frequent	Likely to occur frequently
B Probable	Will occur several times
C Occasional	Likely to occur sometime
D Remote	Unlikely but probable to occur
E Improbable	Highly unlikely

Severity Levels if Nothing Is Done to Address It

Severity Level	Characteristics
1 Catastrophic	Complete organizational loss
2 Critical	Severe injury, major organizational damage
3 Marginal	Minor injury, minor organizational damage
4 Remote	Isolated injury, isolated organizational damage
5 Negligible	Less than minor injury

ity and severity interface with each other. Table 6.2 lets us place these into an assessment matrix.

Determining What Should Be Changed and What Should Be Left Alone

From the matrix, we can discern that not every peril to the organization should be treated alike. Some are more in need of attention than others are. The categories are:

Change should be immediate and
    comprehensive   1A, 1B, 1C, 2A, 2B, 3A

Evaluation should be done to see how
    it could be fixed   1D, 2C, 2D, 3B, 3C

Acceptable with regular management
    attention   1E, 2E, 3D, 3E, 4A, 4B

Acceptable without review   4C, 4D, 4E

Needless to say, great change agents do this kind of assessment in order to paint a clear picture of what the organization is confronting. This enables the great change agent to dedicate their scarce time and resources in a way that leverages their effectiveness within the organization. In other words, it draws the battle lines.

Table 6.2
RISK ASSESSMENT MATRIX

	1 Catastrophic	2 Critical	3 Marginal	4 Remote
A Frequent	1A	2A	3A	4A
B Probable	1B	2B	3B	4B
C Occasional	1C	2C	3C	4C
D Remote	1D	2D	3D	4D
E Improbable	1E	2E	3E	4E

Those issues that are classified as 1A, 1B, 1C, 2A, 2B, and 3A—where change should be immediate and comprehensive—become the focal point for the great change agent. These are the most serious threats to the vitality of the organization. And, consequently, this is where the change agent needs to make their strongest commitment. The second tier—that requires evaluation to see how the problem can be fixed—should be the next series of priorities for the change agent. The last two groups—those that are defined as acceptable—should occupy very little, if any, resources of the change agent.

Again, the idea here is to pick the battles where the demand for transformation is the highest. To squander naturally limited resources on areas that don't mandate the need for action without delay is simply foolish. Nevertheless, this is what happens far too often. Change agents get wrapped up in fighting battles in areas where, even if they are victorious, the impact is barely measurable. The great change agent picks the right fights and manages the inherent risks posed by them.

It is critical that such an analysis is done within context. The introduction of a competitor's new product, for example, may be catastrophic to one company, but just a drop in the pail, or even a benefit, for another.

Derivatives of Managing Risk

Through constant evaluation and re-evaluation of the great issues confronting their organization, great change agents promote an environment that is constantly evolving. Instead of trying to make the organization "settle down"; and seek predictability, order, and stability, great change agents foster an aura that continuously welcomes change. They recognize that turbulence is a fact of life, and deal with it.

By using the above scheme to effectively manage the inherent risk of change, great change agents derive a number of direct, tangible benefits for themselves and their organization.

Managing Risk Allows Focus on External Realities

Managing risk permits great change agents to look beyond their corner of the world and the internal impact of the organization. Instead, they are able to draw the focus of the people toward the external reality of the vision and mission of the organization beyond their "safe" territory.

Managing Risk Provides Signs of Impending Conflict

Managing risk allows the great change agent to deal with potential conflicts in a timely and appropriate manner. The manner in which they deal with a difficult boss, individual and/or organizational fears, and their own personal conduct are just some of the important keys to leading an organization into—and through—the inevitable conflicts of organizational life.

Managing Risk Creates Transparency

Instead of guarding secrets and "scrubbing" data, great change agents are able to demonstrate where vulnerabilities within the organization lie. This not only enhances their credibility, reduces fear, anxiety, and distrust, but also sets the stage to develop an organizational culture in which everyone has both the information to make decisions and to take risks.

Managing Risk Communicates a Sense of Continuity with the Past . . . and Hopeful Future

Great change agents frame the proposed changes in terms of continuity. The goal is not to reject the past. Instead, it's a matter of separating the present from the past without clinging to it. Great change agents are able to explain the past without rationalizing and justifying past errors, which encourages a victim mentality and to describe a vision for the future consistent with the vision of the organization.

Managing Risk Demonstrates Maturity

Because of the knowledge they have accumulated, great change agents project an urgency, passion, composure, and confidence that people will naturally gravitate toward. Even during trauma and stress, great change agents are able to maintain their composure and confidence. Even in the worst of times—and during times of extreme personal weakness, self-doubt, and fear—they are willing and able to draw on the strength of their understanding of what is truly confronting the organization.

Managing Risk Allows for a Consistent, Non-Anxious Presence

To transcend the personal effects of stress in the exercise of being a change agent is perhaps one of the most important skills that one can possess. One uncontrolled outburst, one display of uncontrollable anger can be a very, very difficult thing from which to recover. The process of managing risk gives the great change agent the confidence that what they are doing is right for the long-term health of the organization.

Managing Risk Presents and Holds High the "Big Picture"

Too often, change agents repeatedly and redundantly set the vision of the organization before the stakeholders. If an ineffective change agent cannot put together a practical, coherent "big picture" for themselves, they certainly cannot do it for organizations, either. The managing of risk prioritizes that which is really important and that which isn't.

John Kanas was a schoolteacher who in the early 1970s decided to leave the classroom and enter the world of banking. Over thirty years, he worked his way up the ladder as a change agent and eventually became president of North Ford Bank. Kanas is a firm believer in the concept of managing risk and the benefit it brings in being able to see the bigger picture. Kanas states that most of his time is dedicated to work surrounding the management of risk: "I probably spend 10 percent of my time reading financial reports of the bank and helping to manage the process. I've no time for meetings—never go. Never write memos either. I spend almost half of my day with senior managers and brainstorming business strategies and managing risks."[2]

Those Who Manage Risk Stand Unmoved

In a recent phone call to a colleague, I briefly mentioned, "the new manager appears to be quite good."

"He is," my associate responded. "When he stands for something he stays with it."

Susceptible to fads, opportunism, and expediency, poor change agents may tout the "program of the month," or follow the current "political winds," or the whims of the most influential leader(s) of the moment. Great change agents, however, define themselves and their organization in terms of what has to be changed . . . and they are tough, persistent, and consistent in promoting those ideals. They know there is a cost for their conviction. They know that the hard decisions are the painful ones. Yet, they stand unmoved in the confidence of managed risk. They are able to stand, and stand firm.

Managing Risk and Facilitating Change

When the notion of managing risk is properly applied, there are four principles of innovation that can be used to help facilitate a smoother adoption of change. Those principles are:

The Principle of Relative Advantage

The degree to which a change or innovation is perceived by the members of an organization to be better than the present state of operation is positively related to its rate of adoption. As commonsensical as the principle of "Relative Advantage" may sound, one cannot be "sloppy" or nonchalant about communicating the relative advantages of any proposed changes. This is where managing risk really unveils its benefits.

From the very beginning, it is important that specific, positive, and credible information be provided to the organization, which very simply states how the proposed change is superior to the current conditions. The information must be as believable as possible. The logical progression of managing risk makes this possible.

The Principle of Compatibility

The degree to which an innovation is perceived as consistent and in harmony with the existing values, past experiences, and needs of the potential adopters is positively related to its rate of adoption. The strength and impact of tradition in the life and function of an organization cannot be ignored . . . especially in change processes. Without a continued renewal of tradition, the tenacious hypervigilant guardianship of tradition can strangle an organization's mission and potential. No matter how good their intentions, those who ignore or disrespect these deeply entrenched traditions may become martyrs. Because tradition is such a formidable roadblock to change, change agents are often tempted to "plow through," "buffalo," and stubbornly "bulldoze" their way through the mire and resistance.

The harder they push, the greater the pull caused by later adopters and laggards who become even more determined guarantors of tradition . . . whether the tradition be a building, a way of doing something, technology, product development, etc. It is here that conflict may escalate and intensify. At this point, it is typical for highly sensitive and emotionally charged traditionalists to seek out and support a key antagonist as their "hero" to gather the troops and defend their "cause."

Generally, the "hero" is all too willing to take on the role. Experienced and having successfully offered resistance in the past, the head antagonist will proceed to undermine the proposed change . . . sometimes at all costs. The demonstration of how the change is contrary to the best interests of the organization and destructive of its values often involves the devaluation of those forces promoting the change.

In worse case scenarios, opposition metastasizes the change issue into a personality clash. Name-calling, scapegoating, victimizing, and other destructive behaviors arise, often directed against the integrity of the change agent and those who have the organization's best interest at heart. Sometimes, organizations never recover from the damage. If they do, the scars may still remain for years . . . or decades.

When dealing with the Principle of Compatibility, perhaps the best groundwork for heading off opposition is to initiate a process to define, promote, and celebrate the purpose, vision, philosophy, etc. of that organization. The process of managing risk greatly aids in such a process.

The Principle of Complexity

The degree to which an innovation is perceived as relatively difficult to understand and to use is negatively related to its rate of adoption. If the proposed program has a too-detailed program manual, if it has overly complex timetables, agendas, requirements, multiple manuals, etc., that you can't figure out in five minutes or less, don't give it a second look. It's not worth your time or your trouble. According to the Principle of Complexity, it probably won't work either.

Though detailed materials **may be** needed in backroom planning sessions, the organization **and** its leaders need to have the change presented in the most **simple** and concrete terms possible. People are generally curious about change—whether they are disposed to adopt it or oppose it. The simpler the information, the more clear-cut the proposal, the easier the change and its benefits can be communicated, imagined, experienced, and implemented, and greater the chance of its adoption. The straightforward approach used in managing risk reduces complexity to its lowest possible level.

The Principle of Trialability

The degree to which an innovation may be experimented with on a limited basis is positively related to its rate of adoption. Of the four principles, the "Principle of Trialability" is the most effective and helpful one for facilitating organizational change. This principle recognizes the fact that people are more likely to give a fair judgment to a proposed change if they can see, touch, smell, feel, and experience it first.

Most fear in the change may be due to the fear of the unknown when people feel that they can't go back to the security of the previous state. If things don't work, they become insecure, wary, suspicious, and distrustful. The Principle of Trialability addresses this fear by offering a simple antidote to security: just try it! The formula for managing risk provides us the insight to know what to try and what not to.

Some Final Considerations

Respect timing. Implementation of any proposal, if pursued too quickly or at the wrong time, can quickly become divisive and out of control. If done too slowly, it can lose support and momentum. Timing is, as the old adage says, "everything."

Keep the level of observability of the proposed innovation as high as possible. Publicize and promote it through as many channels as possible. After all, you have nothing to hide! The assuredness in the "managing risk model" provides the security to know that the chosen path is the right one.

Never expect unanimity. In some changes and especially in the trialability stages. Count only the "yes" votes. Let those who want the change support it, move it ahead, and try it. In severely "challenged" organizations, unanimous decisions may be symptomatic of repressing a significant degree of hostile emotions.

There are changes, determined in the "managing risk matrix," like emergency surgery, which must occur. At other times, it may be delayed. In some organizations, those changes that are absolutely necessary may be broken down into incremental steps and patiently implemented over a much longer timetable. We can't always control change, but we can sometimes control the degree, magnitude, and timetable of change.

Especially when going through the process of introducing change, the great change agent maintains their ship to the highest degree possible. They don't get angry. They are patient in public, gentle in private. Most importantly, the great change agent demonstrates character and integrity to all. Managing risk makes all this easier to accomplish.

Chapter 7

Great Change Agents Stoke the Fire of Creativity

Imagination is more important than knowledge.
Albert Einstein

IN NATURE, WE organisms have a tendency to seek balance. We want to adapt to our environment and develop the most efficient lifestyle based on the resources around us. If there is an abundance of a certain hard nut, those with a large, hard-nut cracking beak will survive. If leaves are plentiful at the top of trees, those with longer necks will flourish. Once you reach this equilibrium, you won't have much incentive to continue changing. In fact, change could imperil your success as a species. As a result, evolution goes in spurts of change with long periods of stasis in between.

Our lives work the same way: most of us tend to seek a stable job, a stable community, a regular diet, or a form of exercise. We find a place we like to vacation in, go there every year, and lie in the sun reading our favorite authors. We go to the same church, vote the same party line. We make friends with people who share our interests and settle into regular social schedules with them. We avoid disruption. We shun risk. Deep in our brains, we know that this is the key to survival. Herds only change grazing lands when the drought comes.

There are two results of this type of habitual existence: The first is that we are afraid of trying something new for fear that it won't bring us the same level of reliable reassurance as the things we have always been doing. We don't want to endure the discomfort of failure or even of the unknown. We prefer to limit suspense to Friday night at the movies. Better not to do at all than to do badly. We don't want to stick out and possibly send ripples through the quiet watering hole. I'm not saying any of this derisively; it's a perfectly logical perspective—a perspective the vast majority of people in our society share. The second result is that we are completely unhinged when change does occur. And there is no question that it will occur, it is as sure as summer follows spring, as death follows the cradle.

Thomas Edison was the opposite. Driven to look constantly for desperate needs of the world, he never stopped embracing the inevitable change and looking for new, creative ideas. In 1889, when he was 42, Edison said to a young man of 33, "I would give everything I own to be a young man like you again because there is so much I want to accomplish before I die, and I won't get 1/10 of 1 percent done."[1]

Creativity as an Imperative

America had no real idea how to respond, for example, to the September 11 attacks. There was a real sense of apocalyptic doom after the World Trade Center attacks. It seemed like everything was going to unravel and our entire way of life was done. We were like hens in a coop, completely unable to interpret any howl in the night. Perhaps, that's why we have so many pundits, so many people who reassure us by telling us what is to come. The fact that their collective opinions cover every possible outcome doesn't shake our confidence.

My point is not political. Because, what we really are discussing here is creativity. We must understand that creativity is both essential to survival and is anathema. That's why it can be so hard to overcome the resistance we have to our own creativity. Why does it cause us such a deep sense of fear and dread? Think of the wild architecture that was proposed to rebuild downtown New York in the immediate wake of the attacks. As the dust still lingered, we welcomed a vision of a new world, collective recognition that our times and our landscapes were different. But all too quickly, we became more conservative, more calcified, and the designs morphed back into the predictable visions that suited to calm the public mood. To be creative, you must be brave and allow yourself to take risks. You must also be a little crazy to take these risks.

In the early 1920s and 1930s, cartoons were short interludes shown in theaters before a feature film. Walt Disney had already made his name in these short subjects by employing innovations like sound and color, and by creating the trademark character of a certain mouse. However, sound and color were becoming old hat, and the advent of the double feature meant that there would be less chances for cartoons to be shown.

This was the situation that a young Walt Disney faced. He could have continued on making distinctive short subjects, but he had an idea. His creative vision was an 83-minute cartoon that took years and millions of dollars to make. Many people thought Walt had lost it. People called his absurd idea, "Disney's Folly."

Nevertheless, Disney's vision won the day. In 1937, *Snow White and the Seven Dwarfs* premiered in grand style, bringing audiences to tears. It won Walt an honorary Academy Award.[2]

Change Agents and Creative Perspective

Great change agents have an appropriate degree of perspective when it comes to creativity. They recognize the reason they feel any sort of need to be creative is because they feel some need to adapt to changes in their environment. Their job may be too restrictive. Their relationships may indicate new possibilities. Or, they may just be more sensitive than those around them, a canary in the coal mine, a bellwether to changes that others don't yet sense. Under such conditions, creative change is no longer a risk, it's an imperative.

Nevertheless, great change agents stoke the fire of creativity in a disciplined way. Britannica Online defines creativity as "the ability to make or otherwise bring into existence something new, whether a new solution to the problem, a new method or device, or a new artistic object." It is far too common to observe individuals who have no new ideas and thoughts and do the same thing week after week. Not surprisingly, people will grow tired of it. Any organization and the people who lead it must be creative because people need it. How will any organization grow and mature if it is stuck in a rut?

Most of us have never heard of the IDEO Corporation, but it's likely we've used the products they've designed. From the first commercial mouse, the standup toothpaste tube, and the Palm V organizer to McDonald's 15-second bun-browner, IDEO has been on the cutting edge of business innovation for nearly 25 years. In his best-selling book, *Art of Innovation: Lessons in Creativity from IDEO*, IDEO general manager, Tom Kelley, offers the secrets for stoking the fires of creativity. These secrets could make the difference between business as usual (i.e., you get together every week and talk about the next meeting, collect data, analyze it, and then request more data, etc.) and the business of the unexpected: fresh, compelling experiences with creativity at the core.[3]

Sharpen the Focus

Most organizations use "theme, goals, or objectives" as a focus. While this approach is helpful to give general direction, it is usually a sure way to continue doing things the way you've always done them. That means, for example, keeping the weekly meeting format untouched while throwing in a few "props," such as a team-building exercise.

When the nation's commercial air traffic shut down immediately after the terrorist attacks of September 11, 2001, thousands of families were stranded at the Walt Disney World Resort in Orlando, Florida, unable to return home. Lee A. Cockerell, executive vice president of operations at the resort for the past five years, and his team, after evacuating the park for the first time in its history, made the quick decision to provide complimentary rooms to nearly 7,000 guests. "We immediately suspended all room charges and phone charges," Cockerell recalls. "We gave people money if they ran out so they could eat."

To Cockerell, the incident proved that the creative values he had worked to instill since arriving at Disney World in 1993 had not been ignored. "All the work we did on creativity through the years paid off that day," he says. "We stepped up and did the right thing." "We have a vision statement that talks about making our guests cherished friends," Cockerell explains. "That vision statement is real down here. We try hard to do that. That day we lived by that vision statement. There was never a question of suspending room charges for the people who could not leave. Some people stayed a week. We gave them tickets to the parks for free. "We will never be forgotten for that," he says. "I don't know what it cost us, maybe a million dollars when we were done. But it felt good and felt right."

Cockerell's willingness to take risks, his organizational skills, and his high expectations have contributed greatly to his success, says Wendell Butcher, a friend of Cockerell's since 1981 when they worked together at Marriott. "He's definitely not afraid to take a risk," says Butcher, who is president and a partner in Colwen Management of Windham, New Hampshire, which manages six hotel properties. "In 1986 he and his co-regional vice president took on the objective of upgrading Marriott's food-and-beverage-service delivery in both catering and the restaurants. That necessitated a lot of capital to upgrade from stainless service to silver service and everything that went along with it. They met a lot of opposition, but it was quite successful."[4]

Non-Rigid Rules

If an organization isn't careful, it's easy to kill the creative spirit right out of the gate. Early critiquing and debunking is a sure way to stop the free flow of ideas, and for some reason, many organizations are particularly adept at this behavior. At the start of a new project, we've all heard the comments: "That would cost too much." "It would take too much time." "I live in the real world—this would never work." They might come from well-meaning, conservative participants whose reservations might be helpful in shaping an idea later on, but at this initial stage of the innovation process, these kind of salvos are toxic.

If you ask Linda Doggett about life's biggest lesson, expect to receive a concrete answer. "You don't have to—and shouldn't try to—do it all on your own," says Doggett, associate publisher and creative director at the American Academy of Family Physicians (AAFP) in Leawood, Kansas. "I am surrounded by supportive co-workers, associates, and staff who offer their help. I've learned to take them up on it." That's one reason why she has become so good at what she does.

When she started at AAFP in July 1997 as marketing services manager, the industry was new to her. Creativity, on the other hand, was her best asset. She had made the most of it at two small architectural firms. In between, she did a stint at what is now the International Association of Administrative Professionals, a secretarial organization. There, she acquired skills in membership marketing and program development. The experience enriched her expertise in handling a wide variety of new initiatives from concept to completion. "I have always been drawn to mix problem-solving, creativity and analysis," says Doggett.

Originality comes to the forefront not only in her professional life, but also in Doggett's persona. A few Halloweens ago, Doggett amused herself and her colleagues by wearing violet-flannel pajamas and purple-fleece slippers. She delivered a presentation to honor the one-year anniversary of Holly Sorm, the marketing department's senior project coordinator. "Today would be a good day to wear my pajamas to work," she recalled thinking. "I could get away with that."[5]

Setting Parameters around Creativity

A museum in Corpus Christi, Texas, contains an exhibit of a mockingbird skeleton. Inside the winged skeleton is a huge eggshell. The bird produced an egg too large to lay and died trying to lay it. A change agent who emphasizes or promotes creativity that does not match the conventional wisdom understands how that mockingbird must have felt. When you feel change is needed and seek to initiate that change before bringing others alongside you, then, as the premedieval mariner's maps warned about unknown territories, "There are dragons." People will follow a good change agent almost anywhere when trust is established. And creating trust takes work and time.

Over-ambitious, big-time plans do not always serve the best interests of the organization. In many instances, small is beautiful, beneficial, and better. Management guru, Charles Handy, reminds us that it is often the seemingly insignificant things that alter life most profoundly:

"The chimney, for instance, may have caused more social change than any war. Without a chimney, everyone had to huddle together in one central place around a fire, with a hole in the roof above. The chimney, with its separate flues, made it possible for one dwelling to heat a variety of rooms. Small units could huddle together independently. The cohesion of the tribe in winter slipped way."[6]

Where do you need to build chimneys, rather than bonfires, in the life of your organization?

Chapter 8

Great Change Agents Develop New Ones

Imitation is a necessity of human nature.
Oliver Wendell Holmes

NOT LONG AGO, my senior leadership team and I attended a two-day world business forum in Los Angeles. It was truly an enlightening event. Of the distinguished lineup of speakers, Jack Welch and Larry Bossidy gave us a new insight into managing talent. They both spoke about "human resource." Not in the conventional buzz phrases of "Our people are our greatest asset," but "The **right** people are our greatest asset!" How true this is.

Several years ago, the senior leadership team of our company was listening to the vice president of human resources make a presentation on the management attrition rate. His slide showed that the historical rate had been 6 percent, but in the past year it had increased to 7 percent.

Right away, the whole room equated the current state to be a huge problem, and like most management teams, we began to rapidly toss out suggested actions to address this obvious "horrible situation." As the tempo in this room of 50-plus vice presidents increased to the beat of war drums, one of our team members remained conspicuously quiet.

Finally, after the rest of us had run through the usual solutions with everything from higher pay, to more stock options, to more time off, and more perks—more of everything—he said something that shocked the room:

"The problem with the attrition rate isn't that it is too high, the problem is that it isn't high enough!"

Believe me, that stopped the HR-veep right in his tracks.

The bold executive went on to say, "Based on our current management team's ability, our attrition rate should be closer to 14 percent. The problem is that we are retaining the people we shouldn't and losing the people that should be staying." Even though he made most of us feel pretty stupid, he was right.

No matter where you are in the organization, you have the ability to support change agents in a variety of ways. You can Attract, Enable, Motivate, Reward, and Retain these valuable assets. And this is exactly what the great change agent does.

Ask yourself these four questions—and answer honestly:

- Do you assist in generating or identifying institutional change?

- Do you assist in implementing change by developing proposals or programs to support the change?

- Do you assist in implementing organizational change by serving as a conduit transmitting the virus of change?

- Do you assist in organizational change by adopting the change readily in your department/office?[1]

If you can answer "yes" to two or more of these questions, you are a change agent. And, equally important, you are in the position to develop new ones.

For many successful organizations, the primary management focus is on keeping strong change agents and developing new ones. However, developing new change agents is tough because people willing to be developed are pretty scarce. There are just not a lot of them out there. On top of that, it's tough to build a team with change agents. You can't herd cats, and you can't herd change agents. They are strong-willed and usually have their own vision. Then, if all this weren't enough, good change agents are hard to keep. They will be continually enticed by other opportunities that appear to be more exciting and meaningful.

Investing in people is like investing in stocks. High risk can bring a huge return or a huge loss. The greatest change agents will help you the most but can also hurt you the most. They can leave your organization and go to a competitor. When we embrace people and develop them, we'll sometimes get burned. But still, the future of organizations depends on developing others to be change agents.

Attracting and Keeping Change Agents

At a tactical level, change agents can be attracted from three areas:

First, from managers hired into entry-level or management-trainee positions. People hired for these positions come from a vast array of backgrounds and experiences. They tend not to fit squarely into the mold that we frequently like to have them do—and that is actually a good thing. While the "conventional wisdom" says we should hire business school graduates with such and such GPA, internship experience, specific skills, etc., I find that some of the best change agents and leaders of the future come from non-traditional backgrounds. At the interview level, use that time as an opportunity to see how they react to questions regarding their experience with change in their own lives and those around them.

Second, you can bring in experienced, successful change agents from outside. Needless to say, this will quickly send the message to the rest of the team that change agents are something to be valued and rewarded. As great change agents are always seeking to advance themselves, they are constantly on the lookout for better chances to showcase their skills.

Third, develop the change agents and teams from within the organization. Teams play an integral part in this process, with change agents potentially fulfilling an active formal or informal role in team management or direction. For many organizations, change agents and team builders are intimately connected through a process that includes weekend retreats, monthly breakout sessions at headquarters, and regional seminars across the country. This is done with the goal of positioning the effective change agent within a broader change context that has clearly articulated vision, goals, strategy, and desired cultural values that are continuously communicated and updated to all employees.

Successful organizations understand that organizations are the amalgamation of teams—both large and small—that interact with each other both from within and without. In many ways, the ability of these teams to work together toward a common vision can be the ultimate determinant of success or failure for an organization. Clearly, the ways teams deal with change will have a major impact upon the overall performance of the organization.

Finally, there is a Teddy Roosevelt quote that I have carried with me for many years that embodies much of what a great change looks like:

> Press on no matter what they say to you, it's not the critic that counts, not the man who points out how the strong man stumbles or when the doer could have done better. The credit belongs

to the man who is actually in the arena, whose face is marred by dust and sweat and blood, who strives valiantly, who errs and comes in short again and again, who knows the great enthusiasms, the great devotions and spends himself in a worthy cause, who at the best knows in the end the triumph of high achievement, and who at the worst, if he fails, at least fails while daring greatly, so that his place shall never be with those cold and timid souls who know neither victory or defeat.

Chapter 9

Change Expectations and the New MBA

We aim above the mark to hit the mark.
Ralph Waldo Emerson

IT IS VITAL to create realistic expectations for any change agent and their activities. While it is reasonable to position change agents as catalysts and multipliers of change, they should also not be seen nor view themselves as "walking on water." There is a real danger that they can unwittingly be set up for failure—myopic promises from the senior managers who instigate the change initiative, inflated sense of self-importance from cosseted change agents themselves, resentment, and often downright resistance from co-workers excluded from the program, poor support mechanisms for implementation activities, etc. can each generate a non-conducive atmosphere for change. Simply put, things can go wrong quickly without carefully devised objectives and vigilant control and monitoring. Even with the right players at the table and the resources identified, systems' change initiatives can falter if the change process is not paced comfortably enough to promote ongoing participation and quickly enough to overcome resistance and prevent stagnation. Change activities must also be punctuated with opportunities for both "quick victories" and long-term projects that only yield significant results over time.

Virtually, anyone who has ever worked in a large organization is familiar with the trap of endless processes that produce thick piles of well-intentioned reports but that never really get anything accomplished. It is invariably true that with each new study of a problem, particular members of an organization will learn more about the nature of the issues involved and how best to solve them. This is particularly true where problems and issues cut across multiple aspects of the organization.

There will always be another perspective to consider. Doing "just one more study" can also become a convenient excuse for avoiding action; resistance to change can be easily cloaked in the robes of research and review. However, at some point, it becomes necessary to declare that enough information has been gathered, that no more studies are needed, and that the time for concrete action has arrived.

Helping to identify when this point has been reached and to pivot the organization from contemplation to action is a key responsibility of the effective change agent. The change agent must not only be skilled at the processes required for bringing stakeholders together and finding common ground for problem definition, but they must also know when there has been enough process and discussion, how to move risk-averse or overly cautious players from contemplation to action.

Goals and Objectives in Creating Expectations

Setting goals and deadlines for taking concrete steps is essential. Change agents should agree at the outset on the timelines and event horizons of their collective work, and they should decide in advance when the mobilization of innovative, integrated services will begin. Implementation of change activities will fare better when they are identified as core components of an organization's basic plan rather than a specialized set of activities that managers will get around to when they finally have the time.

My argument is that managing change is really managing others' expectations—shareholders and stakeholders in the firm. Not only do you have to manage those well, but you must also be aware of the limitations of others to manage expectations within their respective organizations. Do not be lulled into a sense of security because you believe you have managed other partys' expectations very well. You must make sure that they too "can and are" managing others' expectations well. Whether it is the CEO or the janitor who cleans your offices, you must understand that each and every individual inside and outside of your organization is managing expectations in their own way with their supervisors, peers, and subordinates.

You must understand that they may **not** be managing expectations well, and in most cases, aren't . . . intentionally. You must make every effort to communicate up and down the organization as well as outside the organization to the various constituencies of your stakeholders if you want to minimize the potential damage from other's inabilities or agendas.

Communicate openly, frequently, and consistently, up and down the various organizations that have stakeholder expectations of you and your firm, and internally within your own firm. Make sure their expectations are in line with reality and are connected to what you have put forward.

If there is mis-management or mis-information behind the scenes by others, this will help overcome "smoke and mirror" problems created by them. Remember, generally, people do not like surprises. Do not "blindside" others, nor be "blindsided" by them, from expectation variances. Manage expectations well for success.

Promoting integration and change is hard work. If all of the goals and objectives identified in an action plan envision changes that will not have an impact on the parts of the organization involved for a long time, the energy and motivation required to make change happen may not materialize. Participants in the change process need to know that what they are doing is making a difference. Creating an integration plan that facilitates a series of early "quick victories" can be very helpful in increasing motivation, participation, and the energy applied to the change process. Achieving these early victories requires participants and leaders to identify programs and tasks that reflect the vision of a common approach to problem solving, which can be accomplished with relative ease and in a comparatively short period of time.

The New MBA (Managing by Accountability)

It is not simply enough to foster an environment that raises up change agents. If change agents are not leveraged and their impact not devolved across the pillars of the company, the culture that produced them will grow stagnant and die. This is where the reward for being a change agent becomes critical.

The word "accountability" in English comes from the 14th-century word *accounts*, meaning a record of money received and paid. King James II of England was the first to publicly use the term accountability. In 1688, he said to his people, "I am accountable for all things that I openly and voluntarily do or say." In short, the word means being answerable for your actions. It does not necessarily mean you will succeed. James lost his throne within a year of making his pledge Nevertheless, accountability offers something better than success. It provides a measure of whether you are doing the best you can in the circumstances—important information, however well you do.

It is because of human nature that we have such a thing as accountability. People are not so committed to a cause that they all just naturally do what they should. Organizations would always be needed (even in a utopian society) in order to work out group consensus on things. But they are needed for more than that. Because of human nature, you cannot count on each member leaving a meeting and all carrying out their responsibilities faithfully. People forget. They get sidetracked. They lose interest, slack off, and just plain shirk their responsibilities. So that is where accountability comes in.

It is the job of accountability to help us overcome human nature, by making us accountable, i.e. putting pressure on group members to each perform their duties. We join groups with an unspoken understanding that the group is going to help us achieve goals that we might not (because of our human nature and lack of discipline) be able to achieve on our own. As long as the goals of the group coincide closely with our own goals, there should be no problems with giving account of our actions. When the goals seem to be quite different, then we leave and go elsewhere.

A successful change agent will choose accountability. To be responsible to others, to allow others to call one to account. An unaccountable person, on the other hand, will answer to no one. The following are some areas of accountability that should be maintained in a change agent's MO:

Integrity of personal life—truthfulness in word and honesty in action. In other words, a high moral and ethical standard of behavior

Integrity of motive—seeking the highest good of the organization before their own benefit

Integrity of relationships—working through conflict and not using one's power to settle personal issues

Integrity of accountability—relationships of genuine accountability must be in place, not merely the form of them.

Legitimate versus Illegitimate Accountability

Accountability is essential for change agents, yet a change agent's accountability can be difficult to structure. At worst, it can turn into a method to control change agents or complain about them. But at best, properly structured accountability does much more good than harm. Sometimes, we chafe under another's accountability simply because we're full of pride. Other times, though, we chafe because we sense something other than constructive guidance being offered. Here are four questions to help determine the legitimacy of the accountability being offered:

- Are they holding me accountable for their personal expectations?

- Are they trying to control me?

- Are they nit-picking?

- Do they have a critical intent?

These types of illegitimate accountability have one thing in common: people assume the change agent's work revolves around their concerns. That is an oppressive assumption to live under.

Fostering Accountability

Change agents need to take positive action to encourage helpful and healthy accountability. Here are four ways to proceed:

Welcome It

We can work to avoid being defensive when people offer suggestions, maintaining an open ear for feedback. When we protect ourselves with defense mechanisms, we become hard, which is too steep a price to pay.

Model It

Holding others accountable requires a willingness to confront others with some difficult truths. At the same time, it models to others how they can hold themselves accountable as well.

Use Opportunities to Teach about Accountability

We can talk about what we are doing and why—what principles are guiding the confrontation. As we discussed previously, effective change agents leverage conflict and misunderstanding as a well-lit stage for instruction.

Never Question People's Motives

Accusations are like weapons of mass destruction; they destroy the entire area in a scorched-earth kind of way. When we wonder what's driving others, we can say, "I may be wrong, but it looks to me like so-and-so happened. Tell me how you're feeling about it." When we refuse to question others' motives, they are less likely to question ours.

Successful change agents will be accountable ones!

Notes

Chapter 1

1. Sarah E. Lockyer, "Julia Stewart," *Nation's Restaurant News* 38, no. 40 (October 4, 2004): 12.

2. Ibid.

3. Charles Fishman, "Change," *Fast Company*, no. 8 (April 1997): 64–70.

4. Philip Dover, "Change Agents at Work: Lessons from Siemens Nixdorf," *Journal of Change Management* 3 (2003): 243–257.

5. Ibid.

6. Peter Schwartz, *Inevitable Surprises: Thinking Ahead in a Time of Turbulence* (New York: Gotham, 2003), 62.

Chapter 2

1. Jeanie Daniel Duck, "Managing Change," *Harvard Business Review*, November–December 1993, 54.

2. Jeff Hiatt and Tim Creasey, *The Definition and History of Change Management* (Loveland: Prosci Research, 2003), 167.

3. Ibid.

4. Ibid.

5. Ibid.

6. "Soccer Mom with Sights on P&G Goal," *Advertising Age* 37, no. 22 (June 2, 2003): 22.

7. Barbara Young, "Sausage Science," *National Provisioner* 213, no. 7 (July 1999): 17.

8. Ibid.

9. Bill McIllvaine, "John Chambers: Cisco," *Electronic Buyer News*, December 18, 2000.

Chapter 3

1. Everett Rogers, *Diffusion of Innovation*, 5th ed. (New York: Free Press, 2003), 145.

2. Liza Berger, "Manuel Gonzalez: With the Eye of a Tiger, This GM Takes Initiative and Sets His Sights on Superb Sales, Service," *Nation's Restaurant News* 38, no. 4 (January 26, 2004): 24.

3. Catherine Marshall, *The Best of Peter Marshall* (Lincoln: Chosen Books, 1983), 120.

4. Ibid.

5. James Gleick, *Isaac Newton* (New York: Vintage Books, 2003), 6.

6. Ibid.

7. Robert Schaffer and Harvey Thomson, "Successful Change Programs Begin with Results," *Harvard Business Review*, January–February 1992.

8. Delroy Alexander, "Brenda Barnes Returns to Corporate Life as Chief Executive of Sara Lee," *Knight-Ridder Tribune Business News*, February 11, 2005.

Chapter 5

1. Peter B. Vaill, *Spirited Leading and Learning: Process Wisdom for a New Age* (San Francisco: Jossey-Bass, 1998), 247.

2. Robert Townsend, *Up the Organization: How to Stop the Corporation from Stifling People and Strangling Profits* (London: Joseph, 1970), 175.

Chapter 6

1. Andrew R. Thomas, *Aviation Insecurity: The New Challenges of Air Travel* (Amherst: Prometheus Books, 2003), 189.

2. "Change Agent," *Long Island Business News*, February 25–March 2, 2000, 5A.

Chapter 7

1. Billy Wireham, "Characteristics of Change Agents," *Vital Speeches of the Day* 65, no. 5 (December 15, 1998): 152–154.

2. Ibid.

3. Tom Kelley, *Art of Innovation: Lessons in Creativity from IDEO* (New York: Currency, 2001), 134.

4. Ron Ruggless, "Lee A. Cockerell—2002 Golden Chain— Executive at Walt Disney World Co. Wins Award," *Nation's Restaurant News* 36, no. 39 (September 30, 2002): 44.

5. "12 Rising Stars," *Medical Marketing & Media* 39, no. 9 (September 2004): 78.

6. Charles Handy, *Gods of Management: The Changing Work of Organizations* (New York: Oxford, 1995), 87.

Chapter 8

1. Tamara Gillis, "Change 101: Back to Basics," *Communication World* 16, no. 5 (April–May 1999): 28.

Bibliography

Alexander, Delroy. "Brenda Barnes Returns to Corporate Life as Chief Executive of Sara Lee." *Knight-Ridder Tribune Business News*, February 11, 2005.

Berger, Liza. "Manuel Gonzalez: With the Eye of a Tiger, This GM Takes Initiative and Sets His Sights on Superb Sales, Service." *Nation's Restaurant News* 38, no. 4 (January 26, 2004): 24.

Block, Peter. *Stewardship: Choosing Service over Self-Interest.* San Francisco: Berrett-Kohler, 1996.

Breen, Bill, and Cheryl Dahle. "Resistance Fighter." *Fast Company*, December 1999.

Bridges, William. *Transitions: Making Sense of Life's Changes.* Medford, MA: Perseus, 1980.

"Change Agent." *Long Island Business News*, February–March 2000, 5A.

Conner, Daryl R. *Managing at the Speed of Change: How Resilient Managers Succeed and Prosper Where Others Fail.* New York: Villard, 1993.

Daniel Duck, Jeanie. "Managing Change." *Harvard Business Review*, November–December 1993, 54.

Donaton, Scott. "Big Business Should Brace for the Return of the Entrepreneur." *Advertising Age*, November 15, 2004.

Dover, Philip. "Change Agents at Work: Lessons from Siemens Nixdorf." *Journal of Change Management* 3 (2003): 243–257.

Fishman, Charles. "Change." *Fast Company*, no. 8 (April 1997): 64–70.

Furnham, Anthony. "Managers as Change Agents." *Journal of Change Management* 3, no. 1 (2002): 21–29.

Gillingham, Andrew. "It's All about Managing Risk." *Business Day (South Africa)*, November 27, 2003.

Gillis, Tamara. "Change 101: Back to Basics." *Communication World* 16, no. 5 (April–May 1999): 28.

Gleick, James. *Isaac Newton*. New York: Vintage Books, 2003.

Hammer, Michael, and James Champy. *Reengineering the Corporation: A Manifesto for Business Revolution*. New York: Harper Business, 2001.

Handy, Charles. *Gods of Management: The Changing Work of Organizations*. New York: Oxford, 1995.

Hiatt, Jeff, and Tim Creasey. *The Definition and History of Change Management*. Loveland: Prosci Research, 2003.

Kelley, Tom. *Art of Innovation: Lessons in Creativity from IDEO*. New York: Currency, 2001.

Kotter, John P. *Leading Change*. Boston: Harvard Business School Press, 1996.

Lamarsh, Jeanenne. *Changing the Way We Change: Gaining Control of Major Operational Change*. New York: Prentice Hall, 1995.

Lockyer, Sarah E. "Julia Stewart." *Nation's Restaurant News* 38, no. 40 (October 4, 2004): 12.

Marshall, Catherine. *The Best of Peter Marshall*. Lincoln, VA: Chosen Books, 1983.

McIllvaine, Bill. "John Chambers: Cisco." *Electronic Buyer News*, December 18, 2000.

Rogers, Everett. *Diffusion of Innovation*. 5th ed. New York: Free Press, 2003.

Ruggless, Ron. "Lee A. Cockerell—2002—Golden Chain—Executive at Walt Disney World Co. Wins Award." *Nation's Restaurant News* 36, no. 39 (September 30, 2002): 44.

Schaffer, Robert, and Harvey Thomson. "Successful Change Programs Begin with Results." *Harvard Business Review*, January–February 1992.

Schwartz, Peter. *Inevitable Surprises: Thinking Ahead in a Time of Turbulence*. New York: Gotham, 2003.

"Soccer Mom with Sights on P&G Goal." *Advertising Age* 74, no. 22 (June 2, 2003): 22.

Thomas, Andrew R. *Aviation Insecurity: The New Challenges of Air Travel*. Amherst: Prometheus Books, 2003.

Townsend, Robert. *Up the Organization: How to Stop the Corporation from Stifling People and Strangling Profits*. London: Joesph, 1970.

"12 Rising Stars." *Medical Marketing & Media* 39, no. 9 (September 2004): 78.

Vaill, Peter B. *Spirited Leading and Learning: Process Wisdom for a New Age*. San Francisco: Jossey-Bass, 1998.

Wireham, Billy. "Characteristics of Change Agents." *Vital Speeches of the Day* 65, no. 5 (December 15, 1998): 152–154.

Young, Barbara. "Sausage Science." *Advertising Age*, January 5, 1998.

———. "Sausage Science." *National Provisioner* 213, no. 7 (July 1999): 17.

About the Authors

M. DAVID DEALY is Senior Vice President of Transportation for Burlington Northern Santa Fe Railroad. A twenty-five-year veteran of railroad management, he has served in top-level positions in operations and marketing throughout the industry, as well as on the boards of several companies and non-profits, including the National Alzheimer's Association. With Andrew Thomas, he is coauthor of *Defining the Really Great Boss* (Praeger, 2004).

ANDREW R. THOMAS is a professor of international business at the University of Akron and serves on the executive education faculties of Management Centre Europe, University of Pittsburgh, and Cleveland State University. He is the author of several books, including *Aviation Insecurity* and *Global Manifest Destiny*, and coauthor, with M. David Dealy, of *Defining the Really Great Boss* (Praeger, 2004).

Printed in the United States
118142LV00015B/32/P